FARE FORWARD:

Letters from David Markson

EDITED BY
Laura Sims

AFTERWORD BY
Ann Beattie

powerHouse Books Brooklyn, NY

TABLE OF CONTENTS:

INTRODUCTION

I first wrote to David Markson in February of 2003. In my impassioned fan letter I said:

> Reading *Wittgenstein's Mistress* was revelatory to me—it rejuvenated my faith in the possibilities of literature. It served as solid proof (ironically enough) that there *was* a living soul out there—someone who was not only trying to "make it new," but who was succeeding wholeheartedly in the endeavor... your work astounds me for the perfect balance it strikes between innovation/art and compulsive readability. In fact, "perfect" is the one word I would choose to describe your work as a whole. Of all the books I've read in the past five to ten years, your latest three novels (*Wittgenstein's Mistress*, *Reader's Block*, and *This Is Not a Novel*) have been the most important and influential to me personally.

I cringe now at the grandeur of my pronouncement—but David wrote me back. He sent me a polite handwritten note the very next day, expressing his "<u>deep</u> thanks" for what I'd written. I was surprised, and consistently thrilled, when we carried on from there—exchanging postcards and letters more and more frequently, warming toward each other, and toward a genuine correspondence, with each one.

When I wrote to David, I would stew over the words and lines as if each note were a crucially worded poem. I even obsessed over which postcards to use—which image would prove how erudite, how cosmopolitan I was? Which image would mark me as the philistine I feared myself to be (at least in comparison with the man who had written *Wittgenstein's Mistress*)? David always sent plain white post office-issue postcards, but I chose ones from an eclectic collection I'd begun to gather expressly for our correspondence; now those cards are accumulating dust in a storage drawer. Sometimes I browse through them and see images I chose with David in mind—Caspar David Friedrich's "Sunset (Brothers)," or an early photograph of Gertrude Stein—and I wish I could still send them to a certain address on West 10th Street.

Our correspondence and friendship spanned the years from 2003 to his death in 2010. It grew through the years, deepening with each letter and card but also, eventually, with several visits and increasingly frequent phone calls. It was an unequal relationship in many regards. David had an illustrious, if underappreciated, writing career behind him (and still before him, as his reputation grew in those final years); I was just beginning to publish poems in a serious way, and looked up to him as a model of what an avant-garde writer should be. We were also, age-wise, at very different stages of life. During those years, David endured various ailments and health scares related to old age, enjoyed the bittersweetness of a last romance, and then suffered its loss. He saw his final book, *The Last Novel*, published, and attempted to escape from what had become his habitual method of composition. During our seven years of correspondence, I got married, published a first book of poetry, lived in Japan for half a year on a fellowship, moved from New York to Wisconsin and back again, published a second book, lost a job I had cherished, and finally, by the time of David's death, was seven months pregnant. Through it all, David's notes punctuated and brightened my life, whether he was chiding me ("Why why why do you do all those readings?"), praising me ("James Joyce…said to tell you, 'Mazel Tov'—which is Irish for 'Zowie.'"), or confiding in me ("I am desperately trying to write a new book."). For seven years he was a great, glowing presence in my life, one to which I turned for literary companionship, mentorship (though he never critiqued my work, except to say it was puzzlingly "difficult"), and also, simply, for friendship.

In 2008, I finally began to come through on the promise I'd made to David early on to spread the good word about his work. I published an essay, "David Markson and the Problem of the Novel" in *New England Review*, and then chaired a panel, "In Celebration of David Markson," at the 2009 Association of Writers and Writing Programs (AWP) conference. Small gestures, ultimately, but public ones at least. I made a recording of the panel for David, and lent him a small tape recorder so he could listen to it—and he did, over and over again, until the tapes wore out. I didn't see the tape recorder again until May of 2010, after months of promises to return it, when David finally sent it back. I hadn't heard from him for a couple of months, but I was too distracted by pregnancy and job-related distress to give his silence much thought. When I got the package, there was no note, which was very unlike David. I called him right away and left a message—was he mad because I hadn't been in touch? Was everything okay? He returned my call later that day, sounding like his jovial self, so I felt reassured—enough to put him out of my mind yet again. Several weeks later, a novelist friend of his wrote to tell me he had died. I was shocked and distraught, and felt that somehow I'd failed him.

This book of letters is not meant to remedy that failure. Nor is it meant to be a comprehensive memorial to Markson the Man or even to Markson the Man of Letters—it reveals a slice of Markson's life, as shared with one person in bits and pieces through the years, but it doesn't reveal, as a lifelong journal or a lifetime collection of letters might, the full arc of his thoughts and feelings, or the full spectrum of his character. The letters here provide a snapshot, not a panorama, but a snapshot is remarkably appropriate for Markson—it gives a narrow, intense glimpse of a man whose work has been narrowly, but intensely adored. It reveals, in its intimate focus, the undeniable vibrancy of the voice of one of contemporary American fiction's greatest innovators—a voice his fans will recognize, and delight in; a voice that will surely delight newcomers to his work as well. In these casually written lines, David's playfulness, his offhand literary erudition, his prickliness and stubbornness, his loving kindness, and above all, his damn good companionship, are on full display. These are attributes of the man that I'm happy to reveal, and preserve, alongside his incomparable body of work.

LETTERS

Feb 4 '03

Dear Laura Sims—

Thank you, and then some, for the kind letter about my work—truly appreciated.

Please do believe that, even though this response won't be half so good as you deserve. Not feeling well here, ergo I've none of the energy it would take to convey how pleased I was—how pleased I *am*—to have received it. I'll reread it more than once, also.

I've heard from the fellow writing the *Review of Contemporary Fiction* essay,[1] actually, but am grateful you're thinking of doing something on my work for some other periodical.

News that may remotely interest you is that I've only lately finished a new book, just now being submitted by the agent. Very like the last two,[2] tentatively called *Vanishing Point*. Whether it's any good or not, however, is another question altogether.

Hey, forgive this, please. As I said, a bum stretch. But I do send you all my best wishes—and again, <u>deep</u> thanks.

Yours—
David Markson

---

1   *Review of Contemporary Fiction*, a tri-quarterly literary journal from Dalkey Archive Press that features critical essays on innovative fiction. Henceforth *RCF*.
2   *Reader's Block* and *This Is Not a Novel*.

Feb 7 '03

Dear Laura S—

A P.S.: I still regret that inadequate answer to your letter. (Whatever it is, here—age, the rotten weather, my 97 sundry infirmities, etc.) But it does occur to me to add: if you ever do write an essay on my work, don't hesitate if/when you have <u>any</u> questions—of <u>any</u> sort—textual, biographical, your choice. Be my pleasure, seriously.

Yours again—
David M.

Incidentally, Astoria[3] is by chance named in my new ms![4]

---

3   My neighborhood in New York at the time.
4   What would be *Vanishing Point*.

Mar 18 '03

Dear Laura S.—

Don't hate me. I just glanced into my new ms for the first time since giving a copy to my agent—and it's not Astoria in there, it's Corona.

Just shows you what us benighted Greenwich Villagers know about exotic foreign territories—alas!

Forgive, eh?

My best—
David

Mar 21 '03

Dear Laura—

Yes, I remember seeing that piece[5]—someone, maybe Bill Kennedy,[6] sent it to me (I have no computer)—and if I'd run into the guy [who wrote it], even in my mid-70s I would have punched him in the mouth. Gawd, of all the naïve, self-contradictory horseshit, full of misreadings, meaningless conclusions, incorrect facts—even insults—well, never mind. (Though in fact I'd still like to whack him one.)

Re the *Newsday* article, only on delayed 2nd thoughts do I remember chatting with the columnist Dennis Duggan, but don't recall ever seeing the piece itself. Maybe looking for it under his name would help you?

Otherwise, again, my best.

Ever—
David

---

5   While researching his work, I'd tracked down numerous reviews and articles online. I'd asked him, here, about one in particular that I'd found to be sloppily written and insulting.

6   William Kennedy, American novelist.

June 5 '03

Dear Laura:

Hey, mazel tov on your good news.[7] Assuming your taste in men is as acute as it is in books, I'm sure he's a winner. My very best to you both.

Even in Wisconsin. Hmmm. I've a vague feeling I've heard that Madison ain't a bad choice. Be happy out there, eh?

Guy name of Jack Shoemaker, who had been the publisher at North Point, and was at Counterpoint when they did *Not a Novel*, has started a new outfit called Shoemaker & Hoard, in DC. They will do my new one next winter, maybe Feb.

Meantime, lissen. Sometime last year I had a note from Ann Beattie, in Key West, saying she was reading here at the 92nd St. Y and that there'd be a ticket left in my name. I didn't get there. A few weeks later I had a dinner date with Kurt Vonnegut and a couple of other chums, and I finked out on that too. But do, as soon as you receive this, scribble me a card with your phone # on same. I will try, try <u>try</u>, to get off my butt and set up a drink or whatever. Honest. (I cannot explain this goddamn reclusiveness, but it's in the last few books, I'm sure.)

---

7   My good news was my impending marriage, and a planned move (from New York) to Madison, Wisconsin.

All congratulations and luck to you both, again.

David

Aug 2 '03

Dear Laura—

I'm sorry, truly. I don't believe I've been any farther out my door than to the local supermarket since my last note. I've just not been feeling well—one damnable medical thing or another. In fact I did not even get to my granddaughter's third birthday party this past weekend, alas.

But I do hope married life goes well. Hell, make that "excitingly."

Likewise for your upcoming move. (Did you know that Leslie Fiedler's[8] PhD was from Madison?) (Heaven only knows how I know it myself, to tell the truth.)

Please do get in touch when you're settled in that other universe. And please accept all my deepest good wishes—to you both—for luck, health, happiness, etc. And (trust me on this) <u>stay young</u>!

Yours—
David

---

8   Leslie Fiedler, noted American literary critic, 1917-2003.

Aug 24 '03

Dear Laura—

Are you really surrounded by water, as on that card? Gee, surrounded by water. Sort of like…hmmm….Manhattan island?

I take all sorts of advantage of it here, too. Back when my kids were about 5 and 7 (they're now 38 and 40) I once took them for a ride on the Staten Island Ferry!

It truly does look spectacular. How'dja know?

Stay well, do well, both of you. (See the last two lines, Part III, "The Dry Salvages.")[9]

All my very best again—
David

---

9   "Not fare well, / But fare forward, voyagers." T.S. Eliot, "The Dry Salvages," *The Four Quartets.*

Oct 1 '03

Dear Laura:

Poor innocent child, thinking a man of 117 years of age would remember <u>what</u> T.S. Eliot quote, that long after I'd sent it. Have you not heard of "senior moments"—or weeks—the current euphemism for rampant senility?

Re your job,[10] Cavafy, a <u>great</u> poet, worked for the Dept of Public Works in Alexandria for 30 years. (That's in my new book. I think it's in my new book.) (Also, that's the original Alexandria, not the one in Virginia.)

Did I say I was 117? Now that the heat/humidity has finally lifted, I sometimes don't feel a day over 109.

Have you guys learned all the words to "On Wisconsin" yet, or just the first stanza?[11]

Hey, again, stay well, etc. Oh, hallelujah—in the context of that last phrase, I just remembered <u>what</u> Eliot quote! So, do so, hear?

Thine—
David

---

10   A temp job I had on arriving in Wisconsin, doing administrative work ("the clerical equivalent of digging ditches/cleaning sewers," as I'd told him in a letter on 9/20/03) for the Fitchburg Department of Public Works.

11   "On, Wisconsin! On, Wisconsin! / Plunge right through that line! / Run the ball clear down the field, / A touchdown sure this time. (U rah rah) / On, Wisconsin! On, Wisconsin! / Fight on for her fame / Fight! Fellows! - fight, fight, fight! / We'll win this game."

Oct 10 '03

Sorry, Ms. Sims—the Lorine Niedecker stuff is in one of my books.[12] I can't remember which, *Not a Novel* or *Reader's B*—but I guess this means your A is now an A-minus.

Industry, extra after-class hours—and neatness—will help.

---

12   In the context of his note about Cavafy (and writers with boring jobs), I'd told him he should include a quote about Lorine Niedecker, Wisconsin poet, in a future novel.

Oct 11 '03

Reader's Block.

Top page 38.[13]

Ha.

---

13   "Lorine Niedecker spent years of her adult life scrubbing floors in a Wisconsin hospital."

Oct 11 '03

*No note, but a neatly excised article from the *New York Times* travel section called "36 Hours in Madison, Wisconsin" that begins, "On an isthmus sandwiched by Lakes Mendota and Monona, Madison, the capital of Wisconsin, is a progressive university town noted for the good life…"

Nov. 8 '03

Dear Simsy[14]—

Hey, thank you for that copy of the *RCF.* I was pleased to see your essay,[15] even though it's hard as hell for me to read same intelligently, what with knowing absolutely nothing about Diane Williams[16]—not having read one word (of her or of anybody else under the age of seventy, it begins to seem). But you make it all about as vivid as it could be under such circumstances. In other words, you write nice. So indeed, yes, I want you "on my side." For that matter, stop threatening and get to it, hear?

Yes, I know about that "other woman."[17] In fact she's already delivered several essays at one conference or another in France. As did someone from Temple U. at an American Lit Ass'n thing in Boston last spring. Plus there's the *hombre* presumably doing the one for *RCF.* So I repeat, kiddo—get to it.

You did see the Markson stuff in a much earlier (1990) *RCF,*[18] no? If we've mentioned this, excuse my ever more pervasive senility, eh?

---

14   This was his first use of this nickname for me; for some reason he alternates, from here on out, between two spellings: "Simsy" and "Symsy."
15   "Diane Williams." *RCF,* Vol. XXIII, No. 3.
16   Diane Williams, American fiction writer, author of *Romancer Erector* and *Vicky Swanky Is a Beauty.*
17   Françoise Palleau-Papin, the French scholar who published *This Is Not a Tragedy,* the first book-length study on David Markson, in 2011 (Dalkey Archive Press).
18   "John Barth/David Markson." *RCF,* Vol. X, No. 2.

Otherwise I wish I had some news—or at least something cheerful to say—but my under-the-weatherness is even more pervasive than my empty-headedness. Just awrful. DON'T GET OLD.

Speaking of which, it only lately occurred to me that tomorrow, around lunchtime, will be fifty years to the hour since Dylan Thomas died about four blocks from where I now sit. He was in a coma for approx. five days, and it was about three before that when I last chatted with him at the White Horse[19] (also four blocks off). But good gawd—a <u>half century</u> ago?! Old, did I say?

Thine—
David

---

19   The White Horse Tavern, at Hudson & 11th Street, was a popular Greenwich Village gathering-place for writers and artists (including David, Dylan Thomas, Bob Dylan, James Baldwin, and Norman Mailer) during the 1950s and 60s.

Dec 4 '03

Dear Laura:

Do forgive the silence. I appear to have gone to 938,627 MDs since my last. No, only a few, just seems that way. // You'd never told me you were a poet, you know?[20] So how'd I know? I sure do wish you luck on placing a book. // I just saw a first pre-pub review of my own new book,[21] only Kirkus, but it appears I am single-handedly keeping American lit significant. I wonder if guys like Roth or Barth or DeLillo know that, poor deluded souls.

Meantime I turn 76 on 12/20. About eighteen months ago I was 27.

Thine—
David

---

20   I had, in my very first letter.
21   *Vanishing Point.*

Jan 8 '04

Dear Symso—

Your cards numbered 1 and 2 actually arrived on consecutive days—in proper order. Occult activity at the PO.

I love it when galleys turn up in bookstores.[22] The SOBs are supposed to be reviewing the books, not peddling them! But I'm pleased you got an early look—and hope you approve.

De Chirico is gone, however.[23] At the very last minute they couldn't get permission. Now a Ross Bleckner that looks like a seersucker jacket that ran in the wash, alas.[24] But some folks seem to admire it, *quien sabe*?

I hope you had a well-celebrated birthday out there (I'm assuming you're back—or surely en route). Thirty's nice, all good things still ahead. (Would you believe Eisenhower was only halfway through his presidency when I hit 30 myself?)

Anyhow, all belated cheers—and my <u>very</u> <u>best</u> to you both.

Thine—
David

---

22   I told him I'd just stumbled on a galley of *Vanishing Point* at Green Apple Books in San Francisco. I was thrilled—he, less so.
23   The copy of *Vanishing Point* I'd found had a de Chirico painting on the cover.
24   The piece is called "The Arrangement of Things (1982)."

Jan 14 '04

Syms-o—

Book en route to you from publisher.[25] Indeed, it may get to you before this card, since with the wind-chill here well below zero, God knows when I'll mail it. Ain't goin' out no matter what.

I'm pleased for you that Review[26] is interested. Write nice. Spell good. Punctuate proper, etc.

And don't comment on the damned misplaced modifier I let go by right at the beginning of the novel—which two beloved chums have already pointed out.

Onward—

Thine—
David

---

25   An official copy of *Vanishing Point.*
26   He means *Chicago Review,* which initially expressed interest in my essay on Markson. I used this early version as a template for the essay that would ultimately appear in *The New England Review* in 2008.

Mar 14 '04

Simsy—

NO, I've no idea what a Blog is.[27] BLOG? Do I want to see printouts or not? Nothing that will upset/annoy/distress me, pls., eh? Only if they <u>truly</u> make nice.

Hey, forgive the brevity, eh?

Thine,

David

---

27   I'd found a lot of interest in Markson on various blogs and had offered to send printouts.

Mar 25 '04

Dear Symsy—

Hey, thank you for all that blog stuff but forgive me if after a nine-minute glance I have torn it all up. I bless your furry little heart, but please don't send any more. In spite of the lost conveniences, I am all the more glad I don't have a computer.

HOW CAN PEOPLE LIVE IN THAT FIRST-DRAFT WORLD?

They make a statement about my background, there's an error in it. They quote from a book, and they leave out a key line. They repudiate a statement of fact I've made, without checking, ergo announcing I'm a fake when the statement is 100% correct. Etc., etc., etc. Gawd.

I have just taken the sheets out of the trash basket & torn them into even smaller pieces.

Last week two several-hour-long hospital medical tests. Plus more MD visits to come. But I am also WORKING. I would rather spend an hour and a half trying to solve the roughest first draft of a note for the new book—that will eventually be endlessly rewritten—than ever ever ever read another <u>word</u> of the Internet.

Don't be sore.[28]

---

28   In my response to this letter, I wrote: "I'm so sorry to have tortured you that

Thine—
David

way—I had second thoughts but went ahead and sent the blog printouts. I have to say it was worth it to get your wittily enraged letter. Those 'semi-literate' bloggers *were* praising you, you know. They did get something right—the most important thing, in fact. Be well and light those toxic shreds of paper on fire if need be!"

Apr 8 '04

Dear Symsy—

Spectacular![29] You can even take the tour,[30] up the rickety stairway to the shabby flat where Raskolnikov did in the old pawnbroker lady and her sister with the ax—and even though there never was a Raskolnikov, or an old lady, or her sister (named Lizaveta), they will tell you, that's the place!

Hey, seriously, I think it's wonderful, a great break from the Amerikansky routine, an experience to feed off for years—even later, when you'll think you've mostly forgotten it. Lotsa pomes[31] too, betcha.

But in the meantime, I demand more and more work on your Markson paper, hear? Every minute, until!

Hey, all cheers, mazel tov, congrats, etc.

Thine—
David

---

29   His reaction to news that I'd be spending a month in St. Petersburg (Russia) as a participant in the Summer Literary Seminars.

30   The *Crime & Punishment* Tour.

31   This is not a typo; he explains the spelling in a later letter.

May 13 '04

Dear Simsy—

Someone just sent me a 90-page densely written Master's essay on *This Is Not a Novel*. Someone else, a Lit Seminar MFA final paper on *Wittgenstein's Mistress*. Yet one more, a chapter on *Going Down*, for a book being done in France.

WORK HARDER! (To strive, to seek, to find—etc. Who'm I quoting?[32])

I don't have any idea whatever became of that essay supposedly being written for *RCF*, by the way. The guy called me with a few questions 15 months ago, but there's been not a word since. I've no idea if it's been written, scheduled—or for that matter abandoned?

When you get to Russia, I want a postcard with a picture of Raskolnikov and the ax on it!

Hey, as always, take care, stay well, and my best to Corey.

Thine—
David

---

32   Ulysses, from "Ulysses," by Alfred, Lord Tennyson: "To strive, to seek, to find, and not to yield."

May 21 '04

Dear Simsy—

Hey, marvelous—that you're essentially finished.[33] I just called James Joyce to inform him, & he said to tell you "Mazel Tov"—which is Irish for "Zowie." Seriously, I'm pleased and honored both—and do hope you place it somewhere prestigious.

Meantime, quote me what it says about Catherine the Great's death[34]—sort of chapter & verse—and I may rewrite & steal it. (I always fuss over sources.)

Again—cheers & congrats—and <u>thanks</u>.

As always—
David

---

33   With my essay on Markson's work.
34   I think this quote about Catherine the Great dying on the toilet came from a Russian travel guide.

May 22 '04

Dear Simso—

Just this a.m., out of the corner of my eye, I spotted a Kate the Great bio on a bookstore shelf—Erickson, was it?[35] Anyhow, I skimmed the necessary pages. Forever on, the line in my next book, if I use the line—and if there is a next book—will be known as the Laura Sims Memorial Water Closet Line!

Thine—
D.

---

35   *Great Catherine: The Life of Catherine the Great, Empress of Russia.* Carolly Erickson (St. Martin's Griffin, 1995).

July 20 '04

Dear Simsy—

Forgive the yeller-paper scrawl. Your cheery, enthusiastic—nay, even bubbly letter—deserves better. And sure does indicate you had a smashing time.[36] Travel's good—says he who once had three years in Mexico, and more than a year and a half in Europe, but lately hasn't been farther away from the Village than Jim Edmonds[37] can throw a baseball. (Then again I've taken the Weehawken ferry a few times, en route to where my son lives in NJ—right past where Aaron Burr shot that guy on the $10 bill.)

Where was I? About to say thanx for the photos,[38] too, making you less than the wraith you've been up 'til now. Corey likewise. I do find it Bishop Berkeley-ish[39] that you visited the houses where two people (three) who never lived, lived. (I say three because Lizaveta was of course the old panwbroker lady's sister; though, hmm, there's RRR's[40] landlady too, no? Tons of people who never lived, lived there.)

A couple of years ago I paused to look at a building on an obscure street not far from here that I'd had in mind, all those

36   In St. Petersburg.
37   Jim Edmonds, retired center fielder.
38   In one photo, I'm standing next to the door of Raskolnikov's supposed apartment; another shows the graffiti scrawled on the wall outside the door of the apartment, including the phrase, "Don't do it, Rodya!" (in French and English).
39   George Berkeley, a.k.a. Bishop Berkeley, a proponent of idealism, the belief that reality consists exclusively of minds and their ideas.
40   Rodion Romanovich Raskolnikov.

decades ago, as the home of my man Chance in *Going Down*; the gal Fern sees him through a window, goes into the building, raps at an apartment door to her left. All these years (earliest drafts, ca. 1960) she's gone into a door at her left. Only in 2003 or so do I discover that everything to the left is another building altogether. To get into the apartment I've visualized her looking into, she'd have to step around the corner! So much for fictional reality!

Golly, what a profoundly metaphysical moment in the creative history of David M—and nobody knows it but Simsy.

Hey, again, pardon the scrawl. Already more'n I'd anticipated.

I'm delighted that you had such a great time. Pomes that you've never given a thought to will be lurking because of it, who knows when?

Thine—
David

P.S. "If there is no God, how can I be a captain, then?" says somebody in *The Possessed*. If there was no landlady on the floor below, who did Raskolnikov owe the rent on his garret to—and what was the exchange rate on the make-believe roubles?

July 25 '04

Simsy—

I have just written nine different drafts—nine—of a roughly 25-word paragraph ending with *Don't do it, Rodya!*[41] Still not right, but now a tentative index card in my shoebox tops.[42] What with Catherine the Great's commode in there already, you may write my entire next novel!

Thine—
D.

---

41   The phrase from the graffiti I'd found outside Raskolnikov's apartment.
42   David composed his last four novels by writing notes on index cards, then filing the cards in shoebox tops, editing the individual notes until he was satisfied, and finally, rearranging the cards until finding the right order. He speaks of this in greater detail during the interview we did for *Rain Taxi*, page 123.

Aug 26 '04

Dear Laura

Thank you

I am pleased to have it[43]

But the poems are so

Difficult

I will try

Some more

Times

Thine

David

(But probably will need more times than that.)

---

[43] A copy of *Bank Book*, my first chapbook of poems, published by Answer Tag Press.

Aug 27 '04

Dear Simso—

Of course you can dedicate that pome to me.[44] I'll be honored.

EVEN IF I DON'T UNDERSTAND IT!!!

Marco Antonio Montes de Oca[45] has a poem entitled "*David Markson ha salido a comprar una botella.*"[46]

By the way, the titles "Bank One," "Bank Two," etc., etc., etc., work well enough—but I assume you're aware there actually is a Bank One? I write them a check every time I pay my Visa card.

Listen, meantime. Eighteen months ago, the guy who was supposedly doing the essay on me for *RCF* got in touch, and we had one phone conversation. Last November, a minor coincidence occurred, involving him—not worth outlining here—but I scribbled him a postcard noting same, also asking what was up with the essay. Silence. Four weeks ago, obliquely triggered by a thought of your work, maybe, I sent another card (this being after another nine months). Again silence. I have no idea what it means—rejected, project canceled, the guy's

---

44   In a letter dated August 24, I'd told him, "When (I won't say if) my manuscript is published in honest-to-goodness book form, I will dedicate 'Bank Four' to you outright. Unless you don't want it!" The poem appeared in *Bank Book*, the chapbook I'd sent him, first, so he had seen it.

45   Marco Antonio Montes de Oca, Mexican poet, 1932-2009.

46   "David Markson Has Gone Out to Buy a Bottle."

moved to Katmandu, whatever? But it may be worth your while to inquire at *RCF* again, if you want. After this latest silence, I thought I'd let you know—with, as I say, no idea what it means or what it's worth.[47]

My old (and in many ways favorite) novel *Going Down* is scheduled to be reissued next spring. Correct that: is <u>being</u> scheduled for then. I exercise caution because it was planned a few times before and always fell into a screw-up.

Otherwise, forgive the scrawl, cheesy paper, etc. For some reason I haven't been able to confront taking the cover off the typewriter for months. Long hours daily here making notes for a new book—but so many damned aches and pains simultaneously that I feel as if I'm 107 years old. Which is pretty grim when you're only 103.

Have you and Corey registered to vote in Wisconsin? (For Kerry, I assume?!)

Thine—
David

P.S. Or re: that other writer, maybe, A., he's just inordinately slow, and B., doesn't answer mail? What I've said is all I know.

---

[47] I did check in with *RCF*. At the time, they said that as far as they knew, the essay was still in progress—though it never did appear.

Sept 30 '04

Dear Simsy—

I am getting so antiquated I cannot remember whether or not I answered your last. Not long ago I spent at least 10 minutes looking for the shirt I'd taken off an hour before—how many hangers and hooks and closets can there be in a one-bedroom apartment?—and then finally discovered I was wearing it!

Who are you again? Who am I writing to?

Lissen, that's lovely news about a NY reading, and I will, will, will try to see you—lunch or something—will, will, will, will, will. Both of you. Will, will, will, will, will.

Rodya, don't do it!

Will, will, will, will, will, will, will.

Thine—
David

Nov 10 '04

Dear Simsy—

Lissen. Re my postcards. See *RCF*, Barth/Markson issue, Volume X No. 2, Summer 1990, Page 158—sixteen lines up from the bottom, the four-word sentence in the middle of the line.[48]

Otherwise, I hope neither of you slashed your wrists after the election.[49] I was gonna jump off the roof here, but my sciatica hurt too much for me to get over the railing.

Thine—
D.

---

48   "He writes only postcards." Beside which I had written in the margin: "Not entirely true!" From the essay, "Markson's New Way," by Burton Feldman, in *RCF*, Summer 1990, Vol. 10 No. 2.
49   George W. Bush was the victor, again.

Dec 28 '04

Dear Simso—

What cozy holiday plans? Reclusive David? Don'tcha read my books?

Betcha didn't know Garrison Keillor mentioned my birthday on the 20th neither! My editor expects an extra sale of at least two copies because of same. Biggest event since my bar mitzvah.

Meantime I hope <u>all</u> your 2005 dreams come true. And I will will will see you when you're here. Will will will will will will will will will will will will.

Hey, be well, both of you.

Thine—
David

Feb 3 '05

Simsy, you're a pisser—

You tell me you'll be in town about 45 minutes, you've got sixteen readings, nine maybe-readings, eleven tentative dinner plans—and I should pick any time that's fine with me!

OK, OK, here's the deal. Sunday, March 6. Noon. Sharp. Place called Rafaella. On Seventh Avenue (maybe it's called Seventh Av. South), just two doors above 10th Street, west side of the street. Name Rafaella on a blue awning (maybe some stripes). Noon gives us comfortable time in which without rush you can leave for that later reading, no? Big, campy joint, two rooms—if you're ahead of me pick whatever location you want—lots with armchairs, even.

But, but, but—do call and confirm when you're here, eh? Sat., or even an hour or two beforehand on Sun. There's one remote (I hope) possible difficulty—and who knows what else, when you're dealing with a 103-year-old wreck?

Done? Done.

Until—
David

P.S. I just may, may still be the guy with the three-month experimental beard—when we are peering around to spot each other.

Feb 14 '05

Simsy, Simsy—

Re "difficulties"—don't forget that I'm probably older than your grandparents! Not to add that I'm beset by 3,724 sundry maladies, likewise. But here, now, two weeks and five days off, looks OK. Fret not.[50]

Meantime, what are all these first-person singulars? Corey <u>is</u> coming, no? (Anyhow, I've got to see how he manages to tolerate you!)

Hey—until—
David

P.S. Yes, dingbat, I know who Jorie Graham[51] is. But I've only known for about 25 years.

---

50   I continued to fret; sure enough, David eventually cancelled.
51   I had a reading with Graham scheduled for the day David and I were supposed to meet.

Mar 22 '05[52]

Simso—

Your card, dated March 12, and postmarked March 14, arrived today—March 21! I'd thought, ah, me, one more lost love!

Hey, thank you for asking about the damnable medical stuff. I've now learned that there is a special seminar in third-year med school, entitled, "How to Scare the Shit Out of Patients," in which my most recent referral MD got an A-plus. But, biopsy or no, I am again given a reprieve. To galumph onward toward senility. Next week: Drooling into my custard.

Meantime I hope I expressed enough delight in the acceptance of your book.[53] It's really spectacular news, and I'm pleased as hell for you. Also glad NY went well, even without grumpy DM.

End space. Too rainy to mail. Hello Corey.

Thine—
David

---

52   On a card announcing the reissue of *Going Down* by Counterpoint in March 2005.

53   I'd recently learned that my first book, *Practice, Restraint*, would come out in October.

May 3 '05

Simso, Simso, Simso—

Lissen, kid, I truly dislike "lunch," part of the total reclusiveness I've fallen into in my later years.[54] I remember Willie Gaddis telling me the same thing, one of the last times I saw him (though I probably didn't understand it yet). So whadaya say to this instead? Why don't you guys stop here at my apartment for an hour or so, in the late morning—say 11 a.m.? That way, you get the whole stretch before your later gig in which to do something far more interesting than watching a grumpy old man dribble egg yolk into his beard (I still have the beard). Eleven o'clock, Sat., May 21.

Done? Done.

But lissen, do, do, do call me earlier—say 9:30 or so, to double-check, just in case. And keep in mind the major sacrifice I'm making—I'll actually have to make a pass at cleaning this place!

Until—
David

---

54   I was going to be in New York again, for another reading, and had asked him to meet for lunch. Again.

52

May 22 '05

Dear Simso—

I'm glad I finally saw you. I am.

Next time I will try to be civilized enough to have lunch, too. And not to spend half our time bitching about all of my penny-ante maladies.

Were I a dozen or fifteen years younger—yeah, say fifteen, so I'd only be 62—I never would have let you go wandering off alone that way either. I did think to check out that restaurant a while later, to make sure you weren't sort of semi-stranded there—after also having paused to discover that that Bowery poetry place[55] was listed in the phone book as well.

I hope the reading was what you wanted.

Meanwhile I keep crossing over to smell the lilacs. I have a vague feeling my woman brings in some in *Wittgenstein's Mistress*, but can't be sure[56]—and haven't opened it in forever. They are now on that small table next to where you were sitting, far more attractive there.

Stay well, both of you.

With love—
David

---

55   The Bowery Poetry Club, where I was reading later that afternoon.
56   "I have brought in lilacs, also." (77)

May 30 '05

Dear Simso—

As you know, I read no fiction at all any longer. But a book I sort of semi-seriously skimmed, because my editor asked me for a blurb, just now out, is *The Method Actors*, by Carl Shuker (Counterpoint, paper)—<u>all</u> <u>about</u> people like you in Japan.[57] Remembered it only after you were gone. Should carry you back, I'd think.

Also, what arrived last week but a check I'd forgotten about—an advance on a <u>Japanese</u> edition of *Wittgenstein's Mistress*. (Don't know when scheduled.)

Lilacs all gone.

With love—
David

---

57   I'd told him, during our visit, that I'd lived in Japan for three years after college.

June 9 '05

Simsy—or rather, Simsy-san—

I don't recall ever having seen a Japanese book but for some reason I'd wager that my title will be: *Wittgenstein's Mistress.*[58]

Why do I think that?

Meantime, if you read that Carl Shuker book, *The Method Actors,* (and who knows, you may be a character in it), do let me know what you think. It will please my editor. And, hell, since they publish W.S. Merwin, Gary Snyder, etc., can't hurt you either, maybe, one day, once I pass it on.

Oh, I forgot. The guy who spoke of "those wonderful folk who brought you Pearl Harbor,"[59] was Jerry Della Femmina[60] (or however it's spelled).

Thine—
David

---

[58]   I'd asked him if he thought there'd be a different title for the Japanese version.
[59]   This was a line he'd quoted to me during our visit, when I'd mentioned my experience in Japan.
[60]   Jerry Della Femina, an advertising executive and restaurateur who wrote a bestselling book in 1970 called, *From Those Wonderful Folks Who Gave You Pearl Harbor: Front-Line Dispatches from the Advertising War.*

June 11 '05

Dear Simso—

I never did mention that poem.[61] The word "stupid" at the end didn't work for me.[62] I tried to think of substitutes, planning to ask you if one of them might fit the translation—that is, if I found one I liked—but got nowhere. But I thank you anyhow. And no, I didn't know it. I know <u>nothing</u> of that literature.

Thine—
David

---

61   I'd included a Robert Hass translation of Kobayashi Issa's death poem in a previous letter to David: "A bath when you're born, / a bath when you die, / how stupid."
62   I happen to love that "stupid" at the end, and told him so in my next letter.

June 23 '05

Lissen, Simser—

What is this wiseguy stuff? If I tell you a poem doesn't work, it doesn't work. Behave yourself.

And what's with Francoise Palleau mentioning that you were here?[63] What am I gonna have to do, demand copies of everybody's e-mail?

Tell Corey, every time you disagree—no question he's right!

Be good. With love—
David

---

[63]   Francoise and I had gotten in touch by e-mail.

July 19 '05

Dear Wisconsin—

Actually there are more than two or three typos in that interview,[64] plus some mis-transcriptions, plus some screw-ups where they cut stuff; but since I do not <u>believe</u> in the web, the hell with it. But aren't you sweet for looking out for me!

Am I supposed to know what PRACTICE [comma] RESTRAINT is?[65] And why isn't there a copy here, stacked between Shakespeare and Dante? Or Homer?

The Danes are great people.[66] When the Nazis in WWII arrived and said all Jews must wear the yellow star, the king himself appeared wearing one.

And then of course there's Hamlet.

(Though of course he's an Elizabethan handover.)

Thine—
David

---

64   I'm not sure what interview he's referring to here, but it must have been an online one I'd found, which becomes clear by the end of the sentence.

65   It was the title of my first book, due out in October of that year.

66   I must have mentioned my brother-in-law, who lives in Denmark with his wife, a Dane.

Aug 12 '05

Simsy, Simsy—

PRACTICE, RESTRAINT is to go between my Shakespeare and Spenser? What am I supposed to do with my Shelley? My Skelton? My Gary Snyder? My Shirley? My Sidney? My Sitwell? My Simic? My Southwell? My Spender? My Karl Shapiro? My Smart? My Snodgrass? My Simpson? My Stevie Smith?

What kind of poet can't even alphabetize?

For shame.

Oct 19 '05

Dear Simso—

It occurred to me later last night that I'd not said congratulations on the book.[67] I've been at it so long that I take them for granted, but I'm sure its existence gave you a thrill—and I couldn't be more pleased for you. Mazel tov.

I also appreciate the inscription—and the dedication on "Bank Four." I promise I'll read it and read it and read it—until I at least <u>begin</u> to understand it.

And the rest of them.

I was delighted to see Corey. He's far too good for you.

Liked your chum Margaret too. You're all so smiley and energetic—gawd.

I kept wondering, when I got home, why I was hungry. Aren't they supposed to give you toast or some such with an egg order—or was it on the side where I didn't notice it?

I also realized I short-changed you guys on the bill. My $20 would have covered my food and drink, but was shy on the tax

---

67   We'd met for lunch (finally, lunch!) earlier that day. I was in town for my book launch.

and tip. <u>DO</u> <u>NOT RETURN</u> <u>THE</u> <u>ENCLOSED</u>![68] (Oops. Tested it against the light. Too visible. I owe you $5.00)

If it arrives. Pretty dumb to send cash in a letter, no?

Hey—I enjoyed it all. And am sorry I don't shut up.

With love to you both—
David

P.S. I also found something to do with the pumpkin.[69] I won't tell. But nice. I even scored points with it.

---

68   There was nothing enclosed, as he explains in the parenthetical remark, which he'd scribbled on later.
69   We'd brought him a miniature pumpkin.

Oct 28 '05

All right, don't ask me what I did with the pumpkin.

You'll never know, now.

[Accompanied by a drawing of a pumpkin, on the bottom of the card.]

Nov 13 '05

Simso—

Down the corridor here, a youngster with fire-engine red hair. When he's carried or wheeled past, he's never done anything but stare and scowl at me. Roughly two weeks ago, near Halloween, he had his first birthday. I knocked—and gave him the pumpkin. Those things are dense, they're heavy. I thought he was nowhere near strong enough, but he gripped it in both hands and wouldn't let go. His mother said he held onto it for days. Ever since, whenever I've seen him, he grins and grins. He's now my little red-headed buddy. And that's the tale of your silly-arsed pumpkin!

Love, etc.—
David

Dec 20 '05

Simso—

<u>You're</u> the one who hasn't written, kiddo. Ever since I told you about the pumpkin. I figured you were sore—a gift from Laura Sims and I'd had the chutzpah to pass it along to a little one-year-old red-headed neighbor, shame on me. No news, in any event. (I have, however, spent more odd moments <u>struggling</u> with your pomes.) Do you know what today's date (above) is?[70] This time, shame on you, then.

Hey, love to you both—
D.

His birthday. His 78th, to be exact.

Feb 1 '06

Simso—

No, I ain't a Capricorn, whatever comes before that—which I recall only because somebody once told me. <u>Don't</u> tell me you believe in that shit?

Gawd, how can you teach as much as you say? The only time I did it full time—1964–66, at LIU—I was semi-suicidal.

Meantime, lissen, you might inquire at *RCF* yet again re your DM essay—telling them you saw a Dalkey Archive catalogue in a bookstore (I'm the one who saw one, but that means they <u>are</u> in distribution) and DM is not even listed for their spring issue. Otherwise, if you don't peddle it before you go to Japan[71] someplace, then what?

Why why why do you do all those readings? Who arranges them? Do you get paid?

Don't leave flowers, telephone.[72]

Old tired sick broke[73]—but with love—
David

---

71   I'd received a writing grant from the Japan-U.S. Friendship Commission for a six-month residency in Tokyo—for fall of 2006.
72   I was going to be in NYC, for a reading again. We couldn't meet but I'd told him I was going to leave flowers on his doorstep.
73   Which would become a primary refrain in his last novel, *The Last Novel*.

Feb 11 '06

Simser—

So I'll never see a Sims/Markson essay in print; ah, well.[74]

Then again, if you'd publish such things, sooner instead of later you'll be Distinguished Prof of Poetry, U of Wisconsin—or wherever—with one class per semester—one semester per year!

And re readings, readings: someone just called me to share an evening (here) with Michel Butor.[75] I said I simply don't, thanx. Only later did I wonder: if they are bringing Butor from Paris, what are they paying him? And me? I never thought to ask. Old-Tired-Sick-Alone-<u>Broke</u>!

Love again—
David

---

74   I think I'd finally told him that I was too busy at the time (teaching 4–5 classes per semester while tending to my own creative work) to finish and send out an essay on his work (which would have entailed rewriting the earlier draft, or starting from scratch).

75   Michel Butor, French novelist, critic, and essayist.

Feb 17 '06

Symsy, gal—

You think you're a poet? Ha, get this. I've just received royalty statements on mine,[76] for Jan '05 through June '05—the usual delay of six months, plus processing. In that earlier six months—a dozen years after publication—I sold SEVEN COPIES! Willie Yeats is turning over in his grave. Eddie Poe weeps where he lies. Johnny Keats whimpers.

SEVEN COPIES! IMMORTALITY.

Ha.

Thine—
David

P.S. You're doomed if you tell a soul!

---

76   *Collected Poems.* David Markson (Dalkey Archive Press, 1993).

Feb 21 '06

Dear Simsich—

A couple of hours after your call—

The total of sales to date[77] (after 11 yrs) is indeed 540! (That's thru June a year ago. Must be as many as 8 since!)

Whoinhell bought 'em?

Love again—and hello Corey—

Thine—
D.

---

[77]   Total number of copies sold of his *Collected Poems*.

March 22 '06

Sims, lass—

So there's Corey, in the new issue of *Fence*—and I learn that his poems are as difficult to solve as yours are. I'm glad. It means you were made for each other!

But I'm sore, too. How come he sez he's reading *Practice, Restraint,* but not anything by Markson? Doesn't he know you're s'posed to?

Then again, somebody else in the back of the book is reading my *Springer's Progress.* Who he, I wonder?

No, I don't subscribe. Someone seems to send it, these last few years.

Nada aqui. Old, tired, sick, broke. <u>But</u> <u>WORKING!</u>[78]

With love to you both—
David

---

[78] On what would be *The Last Novel*.

Apr 13 '06

Simso—

Another periodical that sometimes gets sent to me, & that I merely skim through (DON'T TELL A SOUL!)—*Rain Taxi*. And who's reviewed this month?—my gal Laura! I'm <u>thrilled</u> for you. I mean it. I'm hopping around on one foot as if I have water in my ear. (I also have just had walking pneumonia—but never mind that.) May you have uncountable numbers more!

Why go back to Japan when Minneapolis is welcoming you?[79]

Thine—
D.

---

79   I was about to go there for a reading organized by *Rain Taxi*.

Apr 24 '06

Sims—yeah!

<u>Great review</u>, the Mid-American thing![80] Did you send her a gushing let's-be-friends-forever letter?

In Minneapolis, say hello to Eric Lorberer (Ed., *Rain Taxi*)— (never met—a few brief exchanges.)

For your mystery addiction[81]—Counterpoint are re-doing my two private eye novels[82] (two in one volume), maybe late this year. But you'll be in Japan, no? Too bad, kid.

Hey, love again—
D.

---

80   I sent him a copy of a good review of *Practice, Restraint* that had appeared in the *Mid-American Review*.

81   I was deep into novels by Henning Mankell, Patricia Highsmith, and Ruth Rendell at the time.

82   *Epitaph for a Tramp* and *Epitaph for a Dead Beat*, both highly entertaining and full of Markson-esque allusions.

June 5 '06

Symso, gal—

Donno if I mentioned. Did I say that both of your contributions to my new masterpiece made the final cut?—

A.—Don't do it, Rodya![83]
B.—Catherine the Great dying in the royal W.C.[84]

There are, however, no footnoted citations of sources! And I have no acknowledgments page. But I thank you.

Love—
D.

---

83   "Amid the clutter of multilingual graffiti beside the door to the St. Petersburg garret that is alleged to be the one Dostoyevsky used as a model for Raskolnikov's: Don't do it, Rodya!" (23)
84   "Catherine the Great died after having suffered a stroke and fallen from a commode in the royal water closet." (158)

July 14 '06

Dear Simso-san—

Izzat right? What's "san" mean? (Don't tell me "sir.")

This is the first letter/postcard I've sent to Japan since Doug MacArthur stopped writing to ask me advice.

A very important question. Why, when I wasn't sure on which "Friday," as you put it, you were leaving, and I phoned to say goodbye, did your cheery voice still respond on the machine— as it <u>still</u> does today, July 14, when on impulse, I dialed again? I am not inventing that. Will your "please leave a message" go on for all your sojourn?

Meantime I hope it's all gratifying for you both. My own attitude re Japan echoes Philip Larkin's re your nearby neighbor: "I'd love to visit China, if I could come back the same night." (Maybe he said "same day.")[85]

News, news, do I have any news? The MRI they scared the shit out of me by making me take for my brain did not show a brain tumor (they did not mention whether it showed a brain.) An attractive middle-aged good novelist has proclaimed a desperate crush on me. Temperatures in New York are currently averaging 90+ daily. Tell me your evaluation of Anne Carson. Have you ever read Joanna Scott? What did Materazzi actually say to

---

85   He did.

Zinedine Zidane?[86] Why is Palleau's book now long accepted[87] and there is no word re Sims' essay? Did I tell you about the other young French gal who writes me mash notes? Why, why do I have to be 78—which means halfway through my 79th year? Is there no way to transport every central figure of the Bush administration to Guantanamo in place of 95% of the people there now? Can we ship Scalia, Thomas, Alito, Roberts, along with them? When you come home, will you stop by & put my message on my answering machine with your energetic cheerful voice for me?

I am desperately trying to start a new book.[88]

Love—and to Corey—
David

All of which shows how busy I am between books!

---

86   Refers to a heated exchange that took place between two players during the finals of the 2006 World Cup.
87   Her book, originally *Ceci n'est pas une tragédie: L'écriture de David Markson* (ENS Editions) that would be published in the States as *This Is Not a Tragedy* (Dalkey Archive Press, 2011).
88   One that, he'd told me, he wanted to be structurally and stylistically different from the last four books.

July 26 '06

Simso—Love—

What sort of dummy includes an extra blank sheet in a letter?[89]

No, it is not Joanna Scott.[90] She once worked in my ex-wife/agent's[91] office, and wrote me a lovely (more than lovely) letter re my work more recently, & I finally got around to reading her, which is why I asked your reaction (mine=<u>great</u> prose)—but the one who says she is "besotted" with me is someone else (also good). What is this madness, regarding someone who is exactly (let me calculate), yes, one year, four months, & 25 days short of his 80th birthday! Women are mad (deliciously so, but mad).

Another Country Heard From[92]—great—except if it is all Japan—then, NO. Too real, precise, etc.

I'm glad things seem good—i.e., that your time is <u>your</u> <u>own</u>. There is nothing wrong in using much of it to just sit and stare. And daydream. (Or, even, to recall America from afar.)

---

89   David's letter is written on that "blank sheet"—it came from a typical Japanese letter set, which contains paper, envelopes and stickers, all in a matching cute design. On this one is the phrase: "I want the heart and the strength which became clear like this beautiful sea that continues endlessly widely," along with a picture of a smiling cloud saying: "Hello!!"

90   I was guessing who the "attractive middle-aged good novelist" he'd mentioned as having a crush on him was.

91   Elaine Markson.

92   A title I was contemplating for my second book, which would ultimately be called *Stranger*.

Forgive the scrawl, eh? Again, the humidity is dense enough to swim through. Forgive the prose also, as bad as "the sea that continues endlessly widely." Worse. It is 4:00 p.m. and I am lately half-asleep at this hour. (Even only five years ago I would have revised/rewritten this.)

Yes, the last book all signed, etc. Title: *The Last Novel*. But not scheduled until next spring—probably late spring. I did say my two old private eye things (in one volume) will be out in November, no? Not sure I'm happy re same.

Hey, end of fancy page.

<u>Much</u> love, & to Corey—
D.

Aug 9 '06

Simsy—

Carole Maso I used to know a little, some years back. She's gay.
Indeed, last I knew, she and her partner had a baby.

Joy Williams, very attractive, I met once. She is (was?) married
to the ex-*Esquire* fiction editor Rust Hills. I think they live in
Key West.

Lynne Tillman I never met, never read.

Mona Simpson, likewise.

Christine Schutt—never even heard of.

I'll tell you the truth. It's Emily Brontë.

Lissen, the whole thing is absurd. I've not seen you enough to
have probably mentioned same, but A., I have prostate cancer,
and B., the treatment for same blocks testosterone—meaning I
ain't got no sex life! (Whether I'd have one at 78 in any case is
beside the point.) But all I can do about this besotted lass is sigh
wearily and daydream of the past. I am inordinately fond of—
indeed, cherish—my editor, too, who is in fact younger than the
novelist, recently divorced, now in New York. And tomorrow
or the next day a 22-year-old kid, working on my books, is due
to stop by. And there's Sims, nagging me for a name—when I'm

debating which monastery to enter.

I don't know what became of the Japanese edition.[93] I was sent my few bucks long ago. Usually books eventually arrive. Though it's all sort of meaningless when I can't make sense of them anyhow. I remember tossing out several never-opened Norwegian copies of something, the last time I sold books. They are probably still on some bottom shelf at the Strand.[94]

I was joking about Emily Brontë. It's really Stevie Smith (she did write one novel, no? I delight in her verse.)

In fact it's Jean Rhys. Grace Paley. Angela Carter. Colette.

Greenwich Village streetcorner anecdote for you, circa early 1990s:

Grace Paley: David, how are you? Tell me what's new?
D. Markson: Hi, Grace. Nothing, really. Though in fact I do have a volume of poems coming out.
Grace Paley: That's what we'd all rather do, isn't it?

Markson household anecdote for you, circa whenever she used

---

93   Of *Wittgenstein's Mistress*.
94   The Strand Bookstore, a treasured NYC institution, opened in 1927, the year of David's birth. Located at 12th Street and Broadway, it was one of David's favorite haunts. He sold many books there through the years, and when he died, his library ended up there. One of his fans, Tyler Malone, started a tumblr called "Reading Markson Reading" after David's death. He posts the marginalia found in David's books that Malone and others have retrieved from the Strand.

to spend a week with us, while a client of Elaine's:

Angela Carter never bathed!

Lissen, OK, finally, I'll tell you. It's Anaïs Nin.

Love again—
D.

Sept 5 '06

Simsy, my love—

Okay, I'll tell you. It's Hillary. She's told Bill, and understanding the depths of her passion he's willing to step aside. And of course she'll forgo a run for the presidency.

But don't tell a soul.

What the hell is a "young adult novel"?[95] Don't waste your writing time on <u>trivia</u>, dammit.

Says David—whose two old private eye books will be reissued in a couple of months.

Meantime I love, love, love, your "poet" business card.[96] I would show it to everybody—if I ever saw anybody, any longer. Even had to cancel lunch with my editor, Trish Hoard (of Shoemaker and…) last week, because of awrful arthritis. I'll bet I haven't ever gotten around to mentioning my arthritis—just one more of the 97658 subdivisions of the "sick" in "old, tired, sick, etc."

I wish I had some news. Basically just going nuts, trying to

---

95   I must have told him I was thinking about writing a young adult novel while in Japan.
96   The Japan-US Friendship Commission issued me a box of *meishi*, business cards with English on one side and Japanese on the other, to use during the duration of the fellowship. They read: "Laura Sims, Poet," and listed my Tokyo address. I'd sent one to David.

concoct a new novel <u>different</u> from what I've been doing, getting nowhere—which is to say, doing nothing. Forcing myself to read some of the allegedly "great" novels I've let go past in recent years—Saramago, Sebald, etc., and being bored by all of same. Though Joanna Scott does do loverly prose.

It's not Hillary. It's Beyoncé. Who <u>is</u> Beyoncé?

Re that cartoon I sent[97]—I passed it around a writing class or two—telling them that if they did write, they should be careful whom they marry.

Anyway. Forgive the draggy lack of energy. Not just old, tired, sick, it's old, tired sick, DULL.

But I do send <u>much</u> love—
David

---

97   From *The New Yorker*, it shows a man and woman on a porch; he's seated at a typewriter and she's handing him a sandwich, and saying, "I've got an idea for a story: Gus and Ethel live on Long Island, on the North Shore. He works sixteen hours a day writing fiction. Ethel never goes out, never does anything except fix Gus sandwiches, and in the end she becomes a nympho-lesbo-killer-whore. Here's your sandwich."

Oct 5 '06

Simso—

Okay, I'll finally tell you the absolute, categorical, unadulterated truth. It's Ellen DeGeneres. She's not gay. She's been faking that, so it won't spoil her image when she's seen ducking in and out of my building.

Speaking of in & out of my building, Edie Falco lived here for years, and I had no idea who she was, never having seen *The Sopranos*. (Or maybe it was before *The Sopranos*.)

Forgive the cruddy paper, by the way. (Though at least there ain't no cutesy little pink animals on it!)

Meantime there is NOTHING doing here, still. Awaiting copy-edited ms on the new novel. Lunch with Ann Beattie, dinner with Kurt Vonnegut (and two other chums) being my only recent "literary" activities. Also with my editor and publisher, and my novelist girlfriend (OK, it's not DeGeneres). And she ain't my girlfriend anyhow—though it's nice to have felt a little playfully flirty for a bit, considering all my sexless, energyless ancient debilities. Bright, nice woman.

Still struggling to find something to <u>react</u> <u>to</u> when I read, dammit. About five total Anne Carsons now, and I'm about to quit—an occasional (no, a rare) glittering passage does not a genius make. And all that surface intellectuality is just that, surface.[98] That long Ammons *Garbage* I have tried to get into twice—and cannot believe how it won a National Book Award— via intimidation maybe, a little like Carson in that respect. A Barry Hannah amused me, but wound up with a shrug. A Tabucchi,[99] a grunt. But ignore all this, it's me and my worn-down head, not the books. Or as my once-*Playboy*- centerfold-writer-ex-girlfriend recently said, "David, maybe we've just read <u>enough</u> novels."

Then again, in your honor, I did buy a Penguin Bashō haiku collection. Now that's the stuff for me—eight or ten words at a clip, the entire volume done with in fifteen minutes, hallelujah!

End of page, more than I anticipated. I think I'll consider it a day's work. No, it's Thursday, make it a week's.

Hope you're both OK, still happy there, etc. With <u>much</u> love— David

---

98   I'm a huge Anne Carson fan, and vehemently disagree.
99   Antonio Tabucchi, Italian writer, 1943-2012.

Oct 5 '06

Simsy, my sweet—

A P.S. Correction to this a.m.'s letter. It occurs to me that when I referred to my ex-girlfriend-former-*Playboy*-centerfold-also-a-writer, you might have thought she's the one I've been talking about of late. No, this is another. Was a *Playboy* centerfold <u>when I met her</u>—probably twenty years before yourself saw the light of day. The only centerfold who ever had a short story of her own in the same issue. All these years later, and she lives only about three blocks away here in the Village. Amazing. You turn old and pot-bellied and senile and you're still in touch with some who a half-century ago were heartbreakingly young and beautiful.

Love again—
D.

Nov 17 '06

Simsy my love—

I owe you. But as always, *no hay nada aqui.* I <u>un</u>copyedited my copyedited ms of *The Last Novel*, then proofed the proofs. I get wholly confused re what's what with the two-in-one *Epitaphs* coming out before that. I just had to apologize to that lovely lady French critic for a minor annoying screw-up (mine), and began my letter by saying, "On December 20 I will turn 79. <u>I forget things</u>!" Friends, acquaintances, keep dying (would you believe <u>two</u> memorial services yesterday?) (I went to neither.) (And have long since told my kids—none for me, pls.) Were you aware of the death of Richard Gilman[100] over there—that is, aware that it occurred over there? Another friend (to a small degree).

Yes, no, I am still incapable of reading. Except for Alice Denham's *Sleeping With Bad Boys*, especially all the porno parts featuring David Markson. (Book just now out; she being the ex-*Playboy* centerfold I'd mentioned. Review in this coming Sunday's *Times* refers to "the novelist David Markson ('stud lover boy')." (I kid you not—my step into literary Valhalla.)

Have you heard from Rebecca Wolff[101] re your pomes (as old Aiken[102] used to spell it)? Don't know her, but I seem to receive

---

100   Richard Gilman, a leading drama and literary critic, 1923-2006. He died in Kusatsu, Japan.
101   Editor of Fence Books, who was reading my second manuscript at the time.
102   Conrad Aiken, American novelist and poet, 1889-1973.

a freebee of the periodical now and then. You didn't say where you hoped to land a teaching job; any nibbles?

How odd is it that I know these guys (well, knew, in Dick Gilman's case) with Japanese wives? Pete Hamill & a writer name of Josh Greenfeld being the other two.

But, hey, that reminds me—if you have the odd moment, check to see if a translated *Wittgenstein's Mistress* is in print over there, can you?[103] It's a year and a half ago that I received my few dollars, but I've never seen a book. (I'm not sure why I care; for all I'll know when I do see it, it could be a copy of *The Sorrows of Werther*.) Then again, I could ask the agent's office. If I remember.

Nada mas. My kitchen sink drips. The super fixes it. It drips anew. This comprising the major events in my existence of late.

I will assume you guys are OK. What would happen if I dialed your Madison #? Wait, let me. I just did. It rang & rang. Then, as if an answering machine had been on (but sans message), it said, "Memory full." Is it still yours? Did I ask about this before? On Dec. 20 I will turn 79. I forget things!

But with love—David

---

103   I tried, but failed to find one.

May 21 '07[104]

Simser—

I was amused by that line you changed,[105] which now asks if I sit staring into space on the subway, "lovesick."[106]

You'll get a chuckle in turn when I ask Eric[107] to change the line that follows, from me smacking you upside the head to giving you a whack on the tuchas!

Hey, hope all is well. Nothing new here. (Well, that award.[108]) Reviews <u>very</u> <u>slow</u> in coming in on the new book, but several due soon.

Love to you both—
D.

---

104   I'm not sure why there's been such a long break in our correspondence, though once I came back from Japan, we began speaking on the phone more often.
105   He's referring to a line from the interview, included in this volume, we were doing for *Rain Taxi*. David took the questions I gave him and basically scripted the whole thing, right down to my interjections.
106   I was teasing him about his novelist girlfriend.
107   Eric Lorberer, editor of *Rain Taxi*.
108   He's talking about winning the American Academy of Arts & Letters Award in Literature for "exceptional accomplishment."

Aug 5 '07

Dear Simsy—

Thank you for all the cows.[109] There is now cow flop all over my rug!

Yes, depressed re Brooklyn.[110] Severely. But a lovely letter from Palleau, telling me her husband says it was doomed from the start—since Brooklyn wasn't young enough!

Yes (again), thinking about a next book—but, dammit, collecting these cursed notes again[111]—which (see our interview) I swore I'd not do! Ah, well, keeps me occupied, at least. "Old. Tired. Sick. <u>Alone.</u> Broke."

Some guy who'd wanted to do an interview, and whom I put off, commented on the *Rain Taxi* issue. I told him, "Laura Sims is prettier than you are."

Hey—love to you both—

Ever—
David

---

109   I think I'd sent him a postcard with a picture of cows on it. It's a safe bet, considering I was back in the Midwest.

110   He and his novelist girlfriend, whom he'd code-named "Brooklyn," had broken things off.

111   He couldn't seem to escape his old composition method.

Sept 29 '07

Laura, lass—

November 5th, that 92nd St. thing is. But why in hell would you punish any good friend by making him/her go?[112] A., I'm only one of two readers—Will Self is the other one. B., Ann Beattie is flying up to introduce me, and surely ought to take <u>some</u> of my time. C., with no scenes, events, active moments in my work, I'll surely need at least a 5 min. preface explaining whatinhell the book is all about, and how it works, etc., etc., if what I read makes any sense at all—earlier references to things that now repeat, and so on. Which means your chums will get about a page and a half of Markson for their $18 tickets!

Spare them.

With love—
David

---

112   I'd asked him for the details of his 92nd Street Y reading (his first reading ever, he said) so I could tell friends in New York to go.

Feb 3 '08

Hey—Simsy—

Writing this for your return out there.[113] How great to have seen you. And I'm excited as hell that you'll be <u>here</u> in the fall.[114] (Or, as you suspect, in Brooklyn.)

But, dammit, I owe you a lunch. I started to pay, and you made us split it, and I never thought about my <u>two</u> wines as opposed to your single lovely pale iced tea. Next time on me.

Next time, also, shut me up once in a while, will you? Three hours after I got home all I could still hear was the sound of my own voice.

Incidentally, on the reverse here, now that's the girl of my dreams.[115] Brooklyn who?

Hey—love to you both—
David

---

113   He means my return to Madison—I'd gone to New York for a reading. Again I'm not sure why there's such a long break here between cards, but it could again be because we were talking on the phone more frequently.
114   We'd just learned we'd be moving back to New York, for teaching jobs.
115   He'd uncharacteristically sent me a picture postcard, that iconic close-up shot of a beautiful, green-eyed Afghan girl, taken by Steve McCurry in 1985.

June 9 '08

Symsy—

Blessings on your furry little head for the essay![116] And no need to send one. My buddy Carolyn Kuebler, managing editor up there, has me on their freebee subscription list. (She was with *Rain Taxi* before.) So long as you spelled my name right, what can be bad?[117]

Meantime, lots of medical nuisances here, hospital time (brief), etc. Gawd, I hate being 80! Latest prognosis, fair.

Hey, I'll see you in August. Everything will be better in NY than in Cheese-Land!

Love—
D.

---

116   I'd finally finished and published an essay on David's work. It appeared in the Summer 2008 issue of the *New England Review* and is reprinted in this volume (page 97).
117   He hadn't seen it yet, obviously, and I was nervous for him to read it, knowing he was easily angered by mistakes (as he perceived them) people made when writing about him.

Aug 28 '08

Simsy—

A quick question, at your new address.[118] Why, in your (very good) essay, do you say I called one book *This Is Not a Novel* because a reviewer did?[119] Do I say that, in there? Did I, in casual conversation? I had René Magritte in mind—*Ceci n'est pas un pipe*—and then remembered Diderot—*Not a Conte*—and I'm sure (pretty sure) I named <u>both</u> of those in the text. But not what you say. Just curious, because it made me scowl both times I read it. (I <u>did</u> read it <u>twice</u>, honest.)

Gimme a yell in an odd moment while settling in, eh? Otherwise you are contributing to my increasing senility.

Love again—
D.

---

118   We'd arrived in Brooklyn.
119   This was exactly the kind of response I'd been dreading. At the time, I was positive I had a solid source for that quote—that one reviewer had called *Reader's Block* "not a novel," so David had called his next one *This Is Not a Novel* as a kind of sarcastic response—but now I don't recall what my source was, and I don't remember how I resolved this with David, either.

May 29 '09

Simsy, love—

Will you do me a small kindness, in a spare half-minute? I sent postals to half a dozen of the people who wrote in that notebook you passed around at the AWP panel[120]—most of whom I knew—but wanted to say six words to one other, who gave me only an e-mail address. And me sans computer, of course. Since she'll recognize your name, could you send her 10 words telling her of my backwardness, but that I've wanted to say thanks for her kind note and only this tardily thought to ask you to do so.

I <u>do</u> appreciate it. And now you learn—do Markson one kindness,* and you're doomed to be pestered for others eternally!

With school presumably over, I hope you're writing up a storm. When was that next book due? You guys getting away somewhere, maybe?

Me, I may very well be retired—ex-writer David. Gawd, just awful.

<u>Much</u> <u>love</u> again—
D.

*Rather more than one!

---

120   In February of 2009, I chaired a panel at the AWP conference, "In Celebration of David Markson," with panelists Francoise Palleau-Papin, Martha Cooley, M.J. Fitzgerald, Joe Tabbi, and Brian Evenson. As part of the event, we passed a book of index cards around in which audience members could write messages to David. David had written some introductory remarks that were read aloud, too—page 143.

Mar 7 '10

Hey, Symsy—

Why the hell did I put a "y" in there?[121]

You OK? Seems like back around Christmas or so when I left you a hello on the machine—and no word since. You are, I hope, <u>writing</u>? And both well?

Meantime *nada* here. Everything I can think of would be making me repeat myself—and I almost prefer the silence. (Actually, I hate it.)

Hey, <u>all</u> <u>love</u>—
David[122]

---

121   I'd often wondered that myself!
122   My last postcard from David. We talked after this, though, at least once before he died.

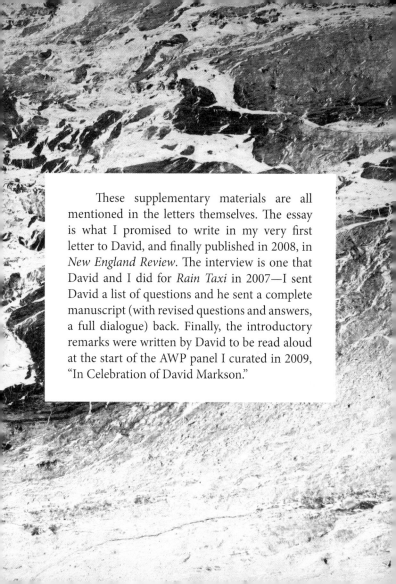

These supplementary materials are all mentioned in the letters themselves. The essay is what I promised to write in my very first letter to David, and finally published in 2008, in *New England Review*. The interview is one that David and I did for *Rain Taxi* in 2007—I sent David a list of questions and he sent a complete manuscript (with revised questions and answers, a full dialogue) back. Finally, the introductory remarks were written by David to be read aloud at the start of the AWP panel I curated in 2009, "In Celebration of David Markson."

David Markson and the Problem of the Novel[123]
by Laura Sims

In Markson's *Reader's Block* (Dalkey Archive, 1996), the narrator asks early on:

> What is a novel in any case? (*RB,* 13)

To which he adds, musing on the work he anticipates writing, which bears a striking resemblance to *Reader's Block* itself:

> Nonlinear? Discontinuous? Collage-like?

> An assemblage? (*RB,* 14)

At the very end of *Reader's Block*, and in the books that follow in this loosely defined tetralogy, including *This Is Not a Novel* (Counterpoint, 2001), *Vanishing Point* (Shoemaker & Hoard, 2004), and *The Last Novel* (Shoemaker & Hoard, 2007), this description reappears, albeit more emphatically; periods have

---

123   This essay appeared in *The New England Review*, Volume 29, Number 3, 2008.

replaced the question marks:

> Nonlinear. Discontinuous. Collage-like. An
> assemblage. (*RB*, 193)
> Nonlinear. Discontinuous. Collage-like. An
> assemblage. (*TINN*, 128)
> Nonlinear. Discontinuous. Collage-like. An
> assemblage. (*VP*, 12)
> Nonlinear. Discontinuous. Collage-like. An
> assemblage. (*TLN*, 8)

And from his latest book, *The Last Novel*, after more than a decade of employing this particular form:

> Novelist's personal genre. For all its seeming
> fragmentation, nonetheless
> obstinately cross-referential and of cryptic
> interconnective syntax. (*TLN*, 51)

Vanishing Point begins with a quote from William de Kooning:

> Every so often, a painter has to destroy painting.
> Cezanne did it. Picasso did it with cubism. Then Pollock
> did it. He busted our idea of a picture all to hell. (*VP*, 1)

And from *This Is Not a Novel*:

> You can actually draw so beautifully. Why do you
> spend your time making all these queer things?

> Picasso: That's why.
>
> …
>
> Writer has actually written some relatively traditional novels. Why is he spending his time doing this sort of thing?
> That's why.

(*TINN*, 156, 164)

All of which would seem to confirm Markson's reputation as a highly experimental, "difficult" postmodern writer "who write[s] writing" instead of stories, and who aims to rebuild the novel, in form and content, from scratch. (*RB*, 163)

What complicates this picture, though, is Markson's undeniable gift for "seducing the reader into turning pages," a phrase we may associate more readily with paperback romances or mystery novels than with serious literature (*TINN*, 3). But Markson, while pushing the boundaries of the novel form, and of contemporary fiction in general, still manages to design characters, stories, and fictional worlds as rich and fully engrossing as those found in more traditional works, however fragmented and unfamiliar these components may appear at first glance. These refurbished versions of traditional elements collaborate with the more easily discernible experimental aspects of his novels to make his work a remarkable hybrid: fiction that is emotionally satisfying, intellectually rewarding, formally distinctive, and compulsively readable all at once.

*

In *This Is Not a Novel*, so named after a review dismissed his earlier book, *Reader's Block,* as "not a novel," Markson's narrator contemplates how the protagonist, Writer, whose style seems to bear a close resemblance to Markson's, aims to bust our idea of a novel all to hell:

> A novel with no intimation of story whatsoever, Writer would like to contrive.

> And with no characters. None. (*TINN*, 2)

> Plotless. Characterless. (*TINN*, 3)

> Actionless, Writer wants it.

> Which is to say, with no *sequence of events*.

> Which is to say, with no indicated *passage of time*. (*TINN*, 4)

> A novel with no *setting*.

> With no so-called furniture.

> Ergo meaning finally without *description*. (*TINN*, 5)

> With no social themes, i.e., no picture of society.

No depiction of contemporary manners and/or morals.

Categorically, with no politics. (*TINN*, 7)

A novel entirely without symbols. (*TINN*, 8)

Ultimately, a work of art without even a subject, Writer wants. (*TINN*, 9)

At which point a quote interjects to disagree:

There is no work of art without a subject, said Ortega. (*TINN*, 10)

Then another quote interjects to disagree with the previous:

If you can do it, it ain't bragging, said Dizzy Dean. (*TINN*, 10)

Insinuating, perhaps, that Writer can "do it," and by association, that Markson can "do it" as well, and therefore is entitled to brag. But we encounter an obstacle to this reading when Writer's existence is called into question:

Does Writer even exist?

In a book without characters?

...

Obviously Writer exists.

Not being a character but the author, here.

Writer is *writing,* for heaven's sake. (*TINN*, 13)

Despite the assertion that he exists as an author, Writer remains confined to the page as a character who is thinking about writing a book, which means that the book we're reading is not, after all, a characterless novel, and does not, therefore, fulfill the standards Writer has set out for his own hypothetical novel. This is the first indication that, however closely it appears to mirror the book Writer hopes to write, one that would destroy all hallmarks of genre, *This Is Not a Novel* remains faithful to certain generic conventions, however unconventionally.

Writer, for instance, is a highly unconventional character.

Like Whitman, he "contain[s] multitudes." Namely: Lorca, Dalí, Chagall, Capote, Sophocles, Kerouac, Corbière, Cato, Melville, Lardner, O'Keefe, and so on. In a feat of intertextual finesse, fragments by and quotes about artists, writers, musicians, fictional characters, and historical figures flit through his head (i.e. across the page), intermingling to tell us who Writer is, what he thinks, feels, and believes, and successfully taking the place of traditional character development. We know, for instance, that Writer is obsessed with death, due to the recurrence of quotes like these:

> Richard Burton died of a cerebral hemorrhage.
>
> Death-of-the-Month Club.
>
> Ensor died at eighty-nine.
> Having done every bit of his significant work before he was forty.
>
> Thomas Wolfe died of tuberculosis which had spread to the brain. (*TINN*, 137)

In order to see Writer as a character, the reader must be willing to fill in the white space around the sparse lines, and find meaning in the juxtapositions, tracking them as they build throughout each book, or even from one book to the next. For instance, Writer's moribund obsession may seem meaningless to the reader who expects a writer to hand him a character's motivations on a platter. Markson expects attentive resourcefulness from his readers, and waits until page 190, the last page of the book, to drop this:

> Writer's cancer.

At this point, only the reader who has actively collaborated with the text will have formed enough of an emotional attachment to Writer to feel gratified, and deeply moved, by this admission and by the book's last line:

> Farewell and be kind.

*

Although *This Is Not a Novel* does not satisfy Writer's genre-busting dreams in terms of character, Markson seems, at first glance, to have successfully discarded plot. Writer's circular thoughts, for instance, certainly do not yield a "sequence of events." However, we find that plots do exist in Markson's work:

> Pliny the Younger was a pupil of Quintilian's.
> Years afterward, learning that Quintilian could not afford a proper dowry for his daughter, Pliny sent the money as a gift. (*VP*, 49)

> E. E. Cummings died after chopping firewood. (*VP*, 106)

> Voltaire's corpse had to be secretly driven out of Paris—sitting upright in a carriage—to be given a Christian burial. (*VP*, 177)

Things *happen* in these quotes; perhaps they happen in miniature, as separate, tiny plots or sequences of action, but these are plots nonetheless, such as: A.) Cummings went out to chop wood and B.) He died.

In both their brevity and their self-contained completeness they are reminiscent of Félix Fénéon's early 20th century *Novels in Three Lines,* each "novel" a tiny summary of a news story taken from the Paris daily newspaper, *Le Matin,* in 1906:

> Le Douz, a sailor, attempted to strangle Mme Favennec, 70, of Brest. When arrested he claimed to remember nothing.
>
> At Saint-Anne beach, in Finistere, two swimmers were drowning. Another swimmer went to help. Finally, M. Etienne had to rescue three people.
>
> Incurably ill, M. Charles Bulteaux opened the veins of his wrists in the woods of Clamart and then hanged himself from an ilex tree. (Fénéon, 49)

Although Fénéon's "novels" do not hang together in the complex, subtly interactive way Markson's fragments do, Luc Sante, in the introduction to the new edition of *Novels in Three Lines* (New York Review of Books, 2007), sounds as though he could be talking about Markson when he describes Fénéon's miniscule novels:

> They demonstrate in miniature his epigrammatic flair, his exquisite timing, his pinpoint precision of language, his exceedingly dry humor, his calculated effrontery, his tenderness and cruelty, his contained outrage. His politics, his aesthetics, his curiosity and sympathy are all on view,

albeit applied with tweezers and delineated with a single-hair brush. And they depict the France of 1906 in its full breadth, on a canvas of reduced scale but proportionate vastness. They might be considered Fénéon's *Human Comedy*. (viii)

Which leads us to consider Writer's intention to write "a work of art without even a subject," "with no politics," and "no picture of society." Do Markson's books adhere to this guideline, at least?

On the foul influence of religion on human nature:

>Burn down their synagogues. Banish them altogether.
>Pelt them with sow dung. I would rather be a pig than a Jewish Messiah.
>Amiably pronounced Luther.
>
>I told you not to go with drunken goy ever.
>Says the ghost of Leopold Bloom's father. (*TINN*, 156)

On poverty (as it strikes artists and writers most particularly) in *The Last Novel*:

>The big tragedy for the poet is poverty.
>Said Patrick Kavanagh.
>
>Try to get a living by the Truth—and go to the Soup Societies.
>Lamented Melville rather earlier. (*TLN*, 132-3)

On the historical role of women in society, particularly in the world of letters (also from *The Last Novel*):

> The greatest achievement for a woman is to be as seldom possible spoken of, said Thucydides.
> Who mentions not one of them in his history.
>
> Johnson's *Lives of the Poets*—which mentions none either. (*TLN*, 107)

A work of art without a subject, indeed.

On looking closer, then, Markson employs many familiar elements of the novel that Writer wants to eschew, but he employs them in radically altered form, which in turn changes the shape of the novel, making it almost unrecognizable to the uninitiated reader. Thus, he still manages to bust "our idea of a [novel] all to hell," but he does so, wisely, without destroying the genre altogether.

Significantly, Writer himself revises his convictions towards the end of the book, as if, in looking back on the previous pages, he recognizes that certain trademarks of fiction may, after all, be unavoidable:

> It is the business of the novelist to create characters.
> Said Alphonse Daudet.
>
> Action and plot may play a minor part in a modern

novel, but they cannot be entirely dispensed with.
    Said Ortega.

    If you can do it, it ain't bragging.

    Or was it possibly nothing more than a fundamentally recognizable genre all the while, no matter what Writer averred?

    Nothing more or less than a *read*?

    Simply an unconventional, generally melancholy though sometimes even playful now-ending read?

    About an old man's preoccupations. (*TINN*, 189)

The Dizzy Dean quote seems muted here, sandwiched in-between these ambivalent revisions. But if what we have witnessed is not, after all, an eradication of the novel form, it is at the very least a significant reinvention, and therefore gives Markson just cause to brag.

*

Form in Markson's novels may be the most recognizably open and experimental element of all. Writer (of *This Is Not a Novel*) lists a set of interesting choices for naming this indeterminate form throughout that volume, albeit in sarcastic response to the reviewer who called *Reader's Block* "not a novel":

An epic poem (*TINN*, 21)
A set of cantos (*TINN*, 23)
A mural (*TINN*, 36)
An autobiography (*TINN*, 53)
A continued heap of riddles (*TINN*, 70)
A polyphonic opera (*TINN*, 73)
A disquisition on the maladies of the life of art (*TINN*, 86)
An ersatz prose alternative to *The Waste Land* (*TINN*, 101)
A treatise on the nature of man (*TINN*, 111)
A contemporary variant on the Egyptian Book of the Dead (*TINN*, 147)
A kind of verbal fugue (*TINN*, 170)
A classic tragedy (*TINN*, 171)
A volume entitled *Writer's Block* (*TINN*, 173)
A synthetic personal *Finnegan's Wake* (*TINN*, 185)

The most appealing and accurate of these may be: "a kind of verbal fugue," and it is one with some history in literature, as Markson himself points out:

The death of Patroclus, *Iliad* XVI:
Even as he spoke, the shadow of death came over him. His soul fled from his limbs and went down to the house of Hades, bemoaning its fate, leaving manhood and youth.

The death of Hector, *Iliad* XXII:
Even as he spoke, the shadow of death came over him. His soul fled from his limbs and went down to the

house of Hades, bemoaning its fate, leaving manhood and youth. (*TINN*, 41)

Each volume of Markson's tetralogy could be described as fugue-like in structure; actual lines, particular sentence structures, or sentences focused on the same subject matter repeat within each book, such as the following from *Vanishing Point*:

> Kuesnacht, near Zurich, Carl Jung died in. (*VP*, 40)
> Rome, Ingeborg Bachmann died in. (*VP*, 45)
> Phoenix, Arizona, Frank Lloyd Wright died in. (*VP*, 49)
> Herefordshire, Jenny Lind died in. (*VP*, 52)

As evidenced by the above quotes, Markson often inverts the natural sentence structure, reversing the order of subject and predicate. In the following lines, in a slight twist on this sentence organization, the predicate comes first in its own fragment, and is followed by the subject in a separate fragment:

> Morningless sleep.
> Epicurus called death.
> …
> An unpurchasable mind.
> Shelley credited himself with. (*TLN*, 116)

> Latin, French, Italian, and Flemish.
> Rubens wrote letters in. (*TLN*, 117)

Apart from helping to create the fugue-like echo, this reversal of traditional sentence structure acts as a tiny suspense-builder, leaving the famous subject's name until the very last, so that our sense of wonder is preserved until the end of the sentence.

The term "fugue" could also apply to the complex threading of lines that repeat exactly or echo one another through all four books, so that each book stands on its own but is clearly part of a larger whole. Because of this, the reader must remain attentive and active when reading the tetralogy, constantly connecting the lines/fragments/quotes not only with their immediate neighbors, but also with lines from previous books, including Markson's earlier works.

For instance, if one has read *Wittgenstein's Mistress* (Dalkey Archive Press, 1988), the book just before *Reader's Block,* one knows that Kate, the narrator, is, or believes herself to be, the last creature on earth.

> In the beginning, sometimes I left messages on the street.
> Somebody is living in the Louvre, certain of the messages would say. Or in the National Gallery.
> …
> Nobody came, of course. Eventually I stopped leaving the messages. (*WM*, 7)

But her loneliness also echoes through the subsequent books, in each narrator's different, but similar solitude:

Nobody comes. Nobody calls. (*RB*, 11)

Someone will call. Surely someone will call. (*RB*, 24)

Nobody comes. Nobody calls. (*TINN*, 186)

Nothing happens, nobody comes, nobody goes, it's awful!
Says Estragon. (*VP*, 68)

Nobody comes. Nobody calls. (*VP*, 162)

Novelist's isolation—ever increasing as the years pass also.
Days on which he is aware of speaking to no one at all, for example, except perhaps a checkout clerk, or his letter carrier, or some basically anonymous fellow tenant in the elevator. (*TLN*, 28)

Nobody comes. Nobody calls. (*TLN*, 56)

Nobody comes. Nobody calls—
Which Novelist after a moment realizes may sound like a line of Beckett's, but is actually something he himself has said in an earlier book. (*TLN*, 58)

For those who have not paid close enough attention. Kate of *Wittgenstein's Mistress* comes to a poignant realization one day:

> ...one curious thing that might sooner or later cross the woman's mind would be that she had paradoxically been practically as alone before all of this had happened as she was now, incidentally.
>
> ...
>
> One manner of being alone simply being different from another manner of being alone, being all that she would finally decide this came down to, as well.
>
> Which is to say that even when one's telephone still does function one can be as alone as when it does not. (*WM*, 231)

As if predicting the narrators of Markson's future, pacing about in their populated worlds, waiting for the phone to ring.

*

But in another sense, Markson's narrators are not alone:

> Rilke wrote standing up.
> Lewis Carroll wrote standing up.
> Thomas Wolfe wrote standing up.
>
> Robert Lowell and Truman Capote wrote lying down.
> Writer sits. (*TINN*, 81)

Voila: a community on the page, one that defies both space and time. Furthermore, Markson, in conjuring this unorthodox community, also creates a great monument to art itself, and to the art-makers who have sustained one another (by criticizing, praising, studying, quoting, and copying one another) through time.

If we consider the books as monuments, then, it justifies Writer's suggestion in *This Is Not a Novel* to call them "Book[s] of the Dead"—especially considering that death is a pervasive focus of the tetralogy.

> Where are those who were in this world before us? Go to the cemetery and look at them.
> Said Anon. in the twelfth century. (*VP*, 183)

And, on opening any of the books randomly:

> Camus died in a car crash.
> …

> Charmian and Iras committed suicide when Cleopatra did. (*RB*, 64-5)

*

> Wallace Stegner died after an automobile crash.
> Bradley died of blood poisoning.
> …

Pablo Neruda died of leukemia. (*TINN*, 104-5)

*

Novalis's *Heinrich von Ofterdingen*.
The last one that Borges asked to hear before his death.

October 17, 1973, Ingeborg Bachmann died on.
(*TLN*, 170)

In absence of an overarching plot, these deaths are crucial events. In most novels, one may find a death or two at the end to neatly tie up a linear plot—but here we have a whole field of deaths on which to gaze, a whole regiment of "linear plots" tidily concluded. One might look at these lines as headstones in a cemetery, which is beautiful in its own right as a work of art, and which appears literally in Markson's *Reader's Block*, as part of the minimal (hypothetical) setting:

Protagonist living near a disused cemetery, perhaps? (*RB*, 14)

Below, Reader of *Reader's Block* considers the blankness of snow covering this cemetery:

With snow, the ranks of still white stone can assume an almost occult unreality. (*RB*, 98)

> Watching abstractedly among the ancient oaks as the entire cemetery commences to disappear. (*RB*, 99)

> The cemetery framed beyond the window in January light. The skull, lower left foreground, a redundant nearer memento mori. (*RB*, 164)

> The eschatology of the still white stones in snow. (*RB*, 165)

What is instantly obvious is the moribund significance of this scene: this is Reader's own end, the erasure of the world, the end of the human race, and of everything.

But Kate of *Wittgenstein's Mistress*, who finds herself truly alone at the end of the world, describes an inherent possibility in the snow's draping effect. Here she depicts the wintertime beach, covered in snow:

> Here, when the snows come, the trees write a strange calligraphy against the whiteness. The sky itself is often white, and the dunes are hidden, and the beach is white down to the water's edge, as well.
> In a manner of speaking almost everything I am able to see, then, is like that nine-foot canvas of mine, with its opaque four white coats of gesso. (*WM*, 37)

What begins as an obliteration of the world by snow, similar to that which takes place in *Reader's Block*, ends with the image of a blank canvas, thus the possibility of new creation. In the next sentence, Kate "draws" on the blank space: "Now and again I build fires along the beach." (*WM*, 37)

She returns to this very description of the wintertime beach towards the end of the book; her attitude towards the scene, however, has changed:

> Still, on the morning after [the snow] fell, the trees were writing a strange calligraphy against the whiteness.
>
> For that matter the sky was white, too, and the dunes were hidden, and the beach was white all the way down to the water's edge.
>
> So that almost everything I was able to see, then, was like that old lost nine-foot canvas of mine, with its opaque four white coats of gesso.
>
> Making it almost as if one could have newly painted the entire world one's self, and in any manner one wished. (*WM*, 233)

It's doubtful that Kate will "paint the entire world [her]self, … in any manner [she] wished"; given her situation, her qualified language is understandable. "Almost as if" and "one could have" indicate her realistic ambivalence about her ability and desire to undertake the task. She has that in common with Reader; both of them lean closer to reading annihilation into the blanked-out landscape, and with good reason. In both characters' cases, the futility of making any new mark on the world becomes overwhelming—why should Kate, as the last human on earth?

And why should Reader, at the end of his life, wholly alone, bother to leave something new behind?

Reader thinks about the end of the world, and about his protagonist courting his own end:

> In the interim, what more for the elderly man in the house at the cemetery but to pause at his accustomed window one afternoon, and gaze for a time abstractedly at the ranks of still white stone beyond, and then turn unremarkably to the gas? (*RB*, 192)

> And as for Reader:

> And Reader? And Reader?

> In the end one experiences only one's self.
> Said Nietzsche.

> Nonlinear. Discontinuous. Collage-like. An assemblage.

> Wastebasket. (*RB*, 193)

Which ends the book and discards it simultaneously, as if Reader, by following his preferred description of the book with the image of the "wastebasket," wipes out the work he has done in one fell swoop, in much the same way that the snow erases the cemetery stones, erasing even the memorial to humankind's presence on earth.

But this reading, despite its negative power, cannot extinguish the possibility inherent in the scene; the snow may appear to erase the headstones, but as we know, it does not: it merely covers them, creating a canvas of sorts, much like the one to which Kate refers in *Wittgenstein's Mistress*. Although neither Kate nor Reader is likely to walk out and paint the world, Markson himself has done so. The very existence of Markson's books indicates that he has committed a gesture of optimism in having walked out and "newly painted the entire world," and will continue to do so, not by erasing the world (of fiction) to start from scratch, but by making bold new marks on a canvas that stretches over the ranks of the dead, the representatives of his human and artistic lineage.

WORKS CITED

Fénéon, Félix. *Novels in Three Lines*. New York: New York Review of Books, 2007.

Markson, David. *Wittgenstein's Mistress*. Normal, Illinois: Dalkey Archive Press, 1988.

Markson, David. *Reader's Block*. Normal, Illinois: Dalkey Archive Press, 1996.

Markson, David. *This Is Not a Novel*. Washington, D.C.: Counterpoint, 2001.

Markson, David. *Vanishing Point*. Washington, D.C.: Shoemaker & Hoard, 2004.

Markson, David. *The Last Novel*. Washington, D.C.: Shoemaker & Hoard, 2007.

Interview with David Markson [124]
by Laura Sims

To many readers, even to those of us encountering it almost fifteen years after its publication in 1988, David Markson's groundbreaking novel *Wittgenstein's Mistress* seemed, and still seems, to have come from literature's future: one that allows for a stripped-down reinvention of character, plot, and narrative while maintaining the emotional intensity and magnetism of the best conventional novels. Markson has refined this alluring combination in the four books that follow *Wittgenstein's Mistress*, each one becoming more and more minimal, thus more and more radical, in their use of the traditional elements of fiction. This loosely defined tetralogy (of which each volume can be readily read by itself) consists of: *Reader's Block, This Is Not a Novel, Vanishing Point,* and, most recently, and the occasion for this interview, *The Last Novel.*

In this latest book, one can detect Markson's singular voice as well as another defining feature of Markson's work: *The*

---

124   This interview appeared in *Rain Taxi*, Volume 12, Number 2, Summer 2007.

Last Novel speaks to its predecessors through a plethora of literary/artistic/athletic/operatic/you-name-it allusions, and through self-reflexive comments on structure, such as: "Nonlinear. Discontinuous. Collage-like. An assemblage." This interconnectedness is most noticeable in the last four books, but one can trace the tendency in all of Markson's books, from the recently re-released early "entertainments," *Epitaph for a Tramp* and *Epitaph for a Dead Beat,* to the more seriously literary *Springer's Progress* and *Going Down.*

Although the mainstream literary world has been far too slow in fully appreciating Markson's work, this May, the American Academy of Arts & Letters honored Markson with an Award for Excellence in Literature. Perhaps it's a sign that the world is catching up, becoming prepared for Markson's inventive fiction; we can hope that his readership will markedly increase as he gains more much-deserved attention. In any case, whether the world-at-large is ready or not, Markson will continue to court innovation in the book(s) that *will* follow *The Last Novel.* As he explains in the interview, he is determined to reinvent his narrative *modus operandi* yet again; *The Last Novel* may mark the end of what has become one of contemporary literature's most exciting and accomplished series of novels, but it marks a new beginning in Markson's endlessly pioneering career.

—Laura Sims

Laura Sims: In *Vanishing Point*, your protagonist speaks about "shuffling and rearranging" his index cards, by way of explaining his method of composition. What does this say about how you yourself go about it, at least in regard to your more recent books? I mean of course those that are crammed with intellectual bits and pieces?

David Markson: It says a great deal, actually. Though in fact my books have always been filled with that sort of material, even if I had to handle it differently, earlier on. Springer, in *Springer's Progress*, Kate, in *Wittgenstein's Mistress*—they're both walking repositories of intellectual trivia. But in those instances, the stuff simply fell as it occurred to them, meaning where it was called for in the narrative. But in these last four volumes—where that material *is* the books—the approach had to be new. All my life I've been an inveterate checker-off-in-margins, but in recent years, writing *Reader's Block* and the rest, I simply began to copy out the stuff that interested me instead. And where better than on three-by-five cards?

LS: But doesn't that become unwieldy? After all, there must be thousands for each book, finally.

DM: Do I describe this or don't I, I can't remember? I file them one behind the other, in the tops of shoe boxes, ultimately two of those taped end to end. So it comes to about two feet per book, I'd guess. But even as the stacks are expanding, I'm shuffling and rearranging repeatedly, as you quoted a minute ago.

LS: Be more specific.

DM: Oh, well—an item about Dante, let's say. If that one seems to go relatively near the front here, then where does this other Dante go? Oh, but now wait, this Guido Cavalcanti on the same theme, which of the two do I connect that one with? And before or after? And how nearby, so the connection might be spotted? Et cetera, et cetera. Obviously, because of the numbers alone, it's far more complicated than that. And on top of which, this is going on for a couple of years also, starting with the lonely very first few cards, and then with each additional one being dropped into one tentative spot or another as I keep on adding.

LS: But even at the end, surely a lot of it still has to be somewhat random?

DM: Of course. There are hundreds of things that I find intrinsically interesting, or that echo different themes, but which have to simply fall where they may. Nonetheless, as I said, those other placements are all generally much more intricate and interconnected than I've indicated, and often pretty subtle. I'm also aware that a fairly high percentage of my readers are conscious of very little of it all.

LS: But good readers are?

DM: Naturally, sure. In fact, an amusing story. Even before he finished the first of them, Kurt Vonnegut called me. "David, what sort of computer did you use to juggle all that stuff?" I had to tell him I didn't own one—I still don't, incidentally—and that it all came out of my aging and rapidly deteriorating brain. Plus of course those ubiquitous index cards.

LS: Why are you suddenly laughing?

DM: More to the same story, actually. That first of the series, *Reader's Block*, is the one in which I mention all those suicides, everybody from Empedocles to Sappho to Hart Crane to Sylvia Plath, there must be a hundred and fifty of them scattered through. Well, and of course also my central figure, Reader himself, at the conclusion. So in any case Kurt called me back a little later, when he'd actually finished. This time it was, "David, I worry about your mental condition."

LS: Presumably you reassured him?

DM: I'm still extant.

LS: But sadly as of recently he isn't, alas. Meanwhile—

DM: Wait. Listen. Under the circumstances, would another Vonnegut recollection or two be out of place here?

LS: Of course not. Do, yes.

DM: Both anecdotes that come to mind involve me anyhow. The first goes back to when I was trying to find a publisher for *Wittgenstein's Mistress*. Or rather when my agent was. Elaine, my ex-wife.

LS: And you had fifty-four rejections. For the work most people consider your most important. It's still beyond belief.

DM: The most dismal part of it wasn't the number of turn-downs, but rather the reasoning behind them. Editors who truly admired the thing, but then announced that it was too intellectual or too offbeat for most readers to handle. Or worse, places where the editor was, in fact, willing to take a chance, but then the sales clucks vetoed it. Trust me, it got to be pretty draining, after a while. This was back in the mid-1980s, by the way. And in any case, somewhere back along in there, there was this major international PEN conference here in New York, writers from all over the world. In recent years I've pretty much ceased to be a PEN member, but at that time I went uptown to sit in on some of the sessions. And at one juncture I was wandering down a corridor in the hotel—I forget which hotel it was—and out of the corner of my eye I spotted Kurt, backed against a sort of cul-de-sac wall, and literally *surrounded* by admirers—at least twenty or more. You know, probably younger writers from everywhere to hell and gone, getting a chance to exchange a word or two with someone they had previously only been able to admire from a distance. Anyhow, I just kept on walking. But then after half a minute, no more, Kurt caught up to me and led me on down the hall—urgently, almost. I don't know what sort of excuse he'd made, to bolt that way. And what did he want? As soon as he found us a quiet alcove—"David, tell me what's happening with that manuscript?" I didn't even remember having spoken to him about the problems. But there he was, that concerned. Now maybe he'd been famous for long enough so that basking in all that adulation was something he could easily wave aside—but still, I found it extraordinary. Who the hell was I? Practically nobody at that entire convention had ever heard my name, at that juncture. But this was Kurt, who he was.

LS: All of us should have friends like that.

DM: But that's part of the point there too. He and I weren't even ever that close, though it would turn out that I'd see a good deal more of him in subsequent years. He was always that way. That second incident I had in mind was only three years ago or so. He was doing a gig at that enormous Barnes and Noble in Union Square. And the place was just mobbed, I mean to the extent that they'd actually had to lock the front doors some hours before it started. I was sitting a little behind and to the side of him, with a couple of others, waiting to go to dinner afterward, and I had a classic view of the kids lined up to get books signed, and it was utterly astonishing. They were being rushed through by the security people, guards snatching their books and slapping them down for Kurt to autograph, no conversation permitted, no requesting please make it "For Evelyn," just snatch, slap, accept it back, and down the nearby escalator you go. But I kept gauging their faces. As I said, again relatively young people, most of them. And it wasn't the predictable look of excitement or admiration you'd see with virtually any other famous author, or even awe, but I swear, there was something almost religious-seeming in it. Is that a ridiculous exaggeration? The more reasonable word I'm looking for is "devotion," maybe. Which probably comes closest to what they felt for him. At any rate, this had been going on for an eternity, and with Kurt eventually in a state of near exhaustion, when a voice came wafting back up from the escalator well, one of the women who'd been shunted down by security: "God bless you, Mr. Vonnegut!" It was unimaginably moving. Not just the sentiment, but the allusion to that title of Kurt's also. Then a while later, when we ourselves were finally leaving—in our case, via an elevator—I asked Kurt if he'd heard it. And when he said he hadn't, and I started to tell him about it, he immediately cut me off. "Wait, listen, that reminds me—" and he commenced to tell me about something kind he'd heard someone say about one of *my* books. How do you match that? Believe me, there may have been better writers in his time than Kurt—well, we know there were—but surely there couldn't have been many more generous human beings.

LS: I'll indicate a short pause here, in the transcript. But let me praise Markson for a moment, too. Why are you so good at portraying women? Not just the two in *Going Down*, or all three in *Springer*—his wife, the one he has the affair with, the old girlfriend who dies—and not even just Kate, whose monologue comprises the sum total of *Wittgenstein's Mistress*. I noticed it even when rereading your so-called "entertainments" recently, more than one in each book.

DM: Thank you. You're sweet too.

LS: Come on, an answer.

DM: I don't have one. I'm pretty sure I was asked that in an interview once before. And all I could say was, could it be because I simply *like* women? Which would mean, I guess, that I pay attention to them. But the gal in my life at the present moment would probably burst out laughing at the notion. She's convinced I no longer pay attention to much of anything.

LS: Don't you? Because that brings me to another question I'd had in mind. You've been quoted as saying you no longer read fiction. Is that still true? And if so, why?

DM: Still, yes. To a great extent. And here again, no answer. Undeniably, some of the most memorable aesthetic experiences in my life have had to do with novels. To make a bad joke, I'm not even sure I ever responded to a woman at the same depths to which I responded to *Ulysses* or to *Under the Volcano*. Or *The Possessed*. But somehow in recent years they just stopped evoking that older sort of resonance for me. Is it age? Is it possible to have simply read too damned many of the things? And a more subtle question here, that equally troubles me. What has my inability to read novels had to do with the way I myself have been writing over that same period, these books in which I leave out so much of the traditional stuff of fiction—plot, background, incident, description, whatever? Again, I'm a blank.

LS: Not to mention you're forgetting an even more critical dimension that you've eliminated.

DM: Meaning?

LS: Meaning character. Wait, here, let me quote. In *Vanishing Point*, you say that you're experimenting—or your protagonist, Author, is doing so—"to see how little of his own presence he can get away with throughout." Why does Author want to remove as much of himself as possible from the book? Or why do Reader, and Writer, and Novelist, in the other volumes?

DM: But isn't the answer in the question itself there, in just the way it's written? Experimenting to see how little of himself "he can get away with"? Or put the emphasis on the word "experimenting." Look, when I wrote *Reader's Block*, the passages about Reader—well, about Reader and/or the character he calls Protagonist, who he's thinking of writing about, but who's obviously an alter ego—that stuff takes up only approximately twenty percent of the book. And the other eighty percent is composed of those intellectual odds and ends we've spoken about, the material from the index cards. That itself was obviously an experiment. But then, exactly as I phrased it— to see what I could get away with—in each of the next three books I held down the references to my central figures to no more than one-and-a-half percent. Honestly, that little. Leaving roughly ninety-eight-and-a-half percent for the odds and ends. But so then what's the ultimate experiment, the thrust of it all? To see if, in spite of that, I can still manage to make Writer and Author and Novelist nonetheless actually *exist*, for whoever's reading me. And apparently they do—the experiment works. Apparently I not only manage to convey a sense of character in each case, but even some dramatic impact at the end as well. And this, again, in spite of there being only that meager one-

and-a-half percent that deals with them directly.

LS: So obviously the index-card material plays its own crucial role also.

DM: Obviously. And not just in the way it's shuffled and rearranged, as we said earlier. That's often just craft anyway, a question of aesthetic balance. Of getting the parts to interrelate, what I label at least once in each book as "interconnective syntax." Or call it poetic structure, despite the fictional length. But what matters even more is the choice of materials. When I'm collecting that stuff, I usually copy out six or eight or ten items for every one I eventually keep. Most of which have to deal with age, death, idiotic reviews, impoverishment, whatnot. It's that which affects that sense of the "portrait" that unfolds— matters that he himself would be preoccupied with.

LS: Death particularly, indeed. Not just the suicides in *Reader*, but then *how* people die, *where* people die, most recently *when* they die. Though with overlapping between books also. Why that central preoccupation?

DM: Hey, Sims, I'm a hundred and nine years old. Can we skip that subject, maybe?

LS: Okay. How about this instead? How does religion fit into your life? Or the work?

DM: Not the most appetizing alternative. I mean since it doesn't, not in any way, shape, or form whatsoever. Yes, there are any number of references to it in the books, but I'm sure you've noticed that every single one of them is negative. Or cynical. Or even vehement, about all the bigotry and hatred and misery and disaster it promulgates—wherever, whenever, any form of it. No, there's no connection with my work at all, certainly no religious impulse behind it.

LS: Another jump, then. A quote from *This Is Not a Novel*: "Photography is not an art." A pretty damning dismissal. And what about film? Does either medium influence you at all?

DM: I've had this argument before. Goodly souls lecturing me about composition, about lighting, all the rest. But in what way does a photograph ever reconceive reality like a Cézanne, say? Or a Matisse? And how can you look at the brush strokes in a van Gogh, or in a Rembrandt—let alone experience the illusion of light bursting out of the pigments in those same very two— and then think of chemically reproduced images on treated paper as genuine art?

LS: Minor art, at least?

DM: Okay, I surrender. But as for film, there again I've never been a buff. And again, it takes a pretty lax definition to use the word art here also. Too many cooks. Romanticism, thy name may be David, but for me art is one poor disaffected wretch all by himself ripping up sheet after sheet in his garret and silently screaming because he can't find that elusive single right word.

Or it's Michelangelo, flat on his back on that scaffolding, month after month, and now and then dropping heavy planks if he suspects the Pope is down below peeping. I'm borrowing from my latest book there, incidentally. But no, I believe no influence from film at all.

LS: Tell me about the internet. Or did we already half answer this, when you said you don't use a computer?

DM: A good deal of what I know about it makes me want to tear my hair. There seems to be no editorial responsibility out there whatever. And no authority, to evaluate things. I don't mean those damned-fool reviews that every dimwit and his cousin Hiram can type in, but even drivel from the so-called Web magazines. Good grief, someone wrote an essay on my work, some few years ago, which I happened to see—a long essay— and the simp couldn't even get the chronology of my life correct, which is readily available. But far more egregious, the piece was patently dishonest. He raised some question or other about what he felt was a major failing of mine, and only at the end did I realize he'd done so without saying two words about one of my most central books, and one which knocked his theory into a cocked hat. Meaning he hadn't even read it. No print editor would have let him get away with that, but here nobody gave a damn. No, I more than realize the conveniences I'm missing, with no e-mail and the rest, but I suspect I'm enduring very little loss in literary terms by going without.

LS: Those two old "entertainments," as you call them—*Epitaph* for a Tramp and *Epitaph for a Dead Beat*—they were recently reissued by Shoemaker & Hoard. Do you really feel that they are mere "entertainments," or do they rise above that self-deprecating title?

DM: Oh, I guess they hold up for what they are, but no, what they "are" are still crime novels, no more. Listen, way back after I did the second one, my agent at the time said the publisher wanted to give me a contract for a series, two a year continually, with the same detective, and even though I was still not getting much serious work done, I dismissed the idea without a second thought. But as I say, I don't disavow the things—in fact I got a kick out of rereading them, after forty-five years—but that's it.

LS: Is there any talk about your satirical Western *The Ballad of Dingus Magee* being re-released?

DM: That would be something else. And after almost the same length of time I'm still pretty proud of that one. I've always felt it's well put together. And everybody found it hilarious—serious-funny, so to say. But then that cretinous Frank Sinatra film sent it eternally down the drain.

LS: Though perhaps with the film so long forgotten someone might take a new look?

DM: Don't transcribe that. People will suspect I asked you to dangle it out there.

LS: All right, another change of subject. Your latest is called *The Last Novel*. Naturally, any number of us hope it isn't that. What's next?

DM: Come hell or high water, it will be different from these last four—the index-card four, as we seem to be calling them. I actually threw in a reference to the word "tetralogy" in this last one, but in all truth I'd never initially intended that. After *Reader's Block*, I simply found myself *addicted* to collecting that stuff. I'd even heaped up those cards with each of the next three before I ever had any definite sense of what I'd do with them— like half molding the flesh before I'd contrived the skeleton to hang it on. But after this last one I forced myself, categorically, to quit. I can stumble onto the most seductive anecdote or quotation in the world, one which normally would have been a spectacular thematic fit for me, and I grit my teeth and ignore it.

LS: Okay, so no index-card material.

DM: Actually, the basic form will probably be somewhat the same, still "experimental" in that way. Short takes as opposed to lengthy narrative, no fictional baggage, no dramatic scenes, no episodes, and many of what we've been calling odds and ends coming from an actual relationship itself. But it's all extremely tentative in my head still.

LS: But you used the word "relationship." You mean a novel about *people*, plural, instead of merely the isolated single individuals you've been dealing with? And not just in these four titles, but as long ago as in *Wittgenstein's Mistress* as well?

DM: Yes. A man and a woman. A guy and a gal. Him, her. Them.

LS: I'm noticing that twinkle in your eye. You're not by any chance talking about a love story?

DM: Who? Didn't I tell you I'm a hundred and nine years old?

LS: You're only seventy-nine.

DM: And devious, too. When else would you be tricked into calling someone "only" seventy-nine, except after he'd said he was that much older?

LS: I'm not forgetting that you also just now referred to a woman in your life. Which reminds me that I'd been intending to ask you about your reputation as an archetypal sort of recluse. May I presume you're no longer quite that?

DM: She lives in Park Slope, in Brooklyn. It's forty minutes, from here in Greenwich Village.

LS: Not a bad commute, especially considering the journey's end. Do you read on the subway? Or just stare into space, lovesick?

DM: Can you indicate at this point that I just smacked you upside the head? Ask me something absolutely unrelated, you hear?

LS: Maybe not wholly unrelated. Since you want to smack somebody, tell me if you ever had a fistfight.

DM: Good lord. Though as a matter of fact, yes. Once. When I was about thirteen. For what seemed like practically an hour. Back and forth across front lawns, in and out of driveways, between parked cars—neither one of us willing to quit. This being back in Albany, where I grew up. Finally a couple of the older kids who'd been egging us on called it a draw. But what I'd not been aware of, and nobody'd said a word about, was that the other boy was wearing a ring. My face wound up looking as if I'd fallen under the proverbial lawn mower. I was reluctant to go to school for days.

LS: What is that new look of delight, suddenly?

DM: I only this instant realize. Ask me an irrelevant question and it turns out to have a literary connection after all. The very kid I fought with is quoted in my latest book.

LS: You're not serious?

DM: Fact. We went on through high school together, and after that I think I saw him no more than two or three times, and not since around the Kennedy years. But lately he's phoned me now and then. And somehow he stumbled onto one of the books, maybe *Vanishing Point*. How, I've no idea, since he turns out to be unquestionably not a reader. But he called me about it.

LS: And?

DM: I quote him without any sort of attribution, just the few words, in an isolated paragraph. He doesn't even quite sense what he's saying, or certainly not who he's saying it to, meaning the *author*, but it's extraordinarily appropriate to all the other typical dunderheaded critical put-downs of everybody that I make use of all the way through. The passage that says, "Listen, I bought your latest book. But I quit after six pages. That's all there is, those little things?"

LS: Oh god—what did you tell him?

DM: What could I say? Something like, "Yes, that's all there is, those little things."

LS: David, there's more. Believe me, there's rather more.

DM: Hey, I know. But thank you.

<u>"In Celebration of David Markson," AWP Conference, Chicago, February 2009</u>

David's introductory remarks, read aloud by Martha Cooley to the fifty-plus audience members:

From David Markson, in New York—

Just a few words of greeting—and regrets that I can't be there, if only to lurk anonymously in a back corner.

To Laura Sims, a good buddy—and a good poet—even if I sometimes can't understand half of what she writes.

To Francoise Palleau, a dear friend, who's lucky I'm not 65 years younger—or I'd be chasing after <u>both</u> of her gorgeous daughters.

To Joe Tabbi, with whom I go back at least twenty years—even if he seems to have lost my address and phone number in the last several.

To Maria Fitzgerald and Brian Evenson, regrettably, neither of whom I've met. But, hell, I'm only 81—there's plenty of time.

To Martha Cooley, with whom I've shared endless laughter—except when she's proclaiming in despair, "David, you've told me that—three times, already!"

And to the audience, all two or three of you. It's been a long haul for me to get to where things like this happen, but that only makes it all the more gratifying. My very best—and my thanks for your interest.

But one more moment, if I may, a note of an entirely different sort. If anyone is ever doing any work involving my novel *Reader's Block*—writing about it—please, please, use the latest edition, the one with the blue-ish gray cover marked 3rd printing, 2007. Because of a horror story I won't go into here, the 2nd printing, the one dated 2001—for years the most commonly available one—contains endless <u>egregious</u> errors. To this day I don't know why I'm not serving 20 years to life for having committed homicide because of it. Again, please, quote only the 2007 edition—i.e., the one dated nearest to the time when you're hearing this—which I believe is fully corrected. Thank you again.

David Markson
by Ann Beattie

Of course I never thought I'd be writing about David Markson when he was no longer with us. I should have done it when he was alive, wondering in his bemused way if anyone who lived in his Greenwich Village apartment had any idea Writer lived in the building, let alone when his *birthday* was. I wrote a blurb for one of his books, and I had the honor of introducing him in his only reading at the 92nd Street Y, but in between times we just made plans to get together when I returned to the city, saying *maybe*, meeting—if it worked out— at a restaurant close to his apartment. A glass of wine at lunch, what the hell! And a steak to go with that. He absolutely would not let me pick him up by cab or car service the night he was reading at the Y, insisting he'd take the subway. He did let me hail a cab back to my hotel afterwards, and he came with me and had a drink at the bar, insisting he'd take the subway back to West 10th. You can't do anything with people. He was set in his ways, but he liked his routines, his patterns, his freedom. Sometimes not spending money equals freedom, at least to a certain way of thinking: you're not beholden; you're used to the silence and the lack of eye contact on the subway, and who wants to have to sit in strained silence with a driver you don't know? He had no cell phone to consult in the back seat. He probably wouldn't have known the etiquette about opening a bottle of water. In a cab, he'd have had to listen to the cab driver speaking to someone in another language, or he might have been consulted about his preferred route home when, like any intelligent New Yorker, he knew whatever he said would only result in absolving the cab driver of responsibility if the street was blocked off because a movie was being shot, or if there was a bulldozer in the middle of Sixth Avenue, which no one local *ever* called "The Avenue of the Americas."

Never mind what we talked about at the bar. And forgive me for letting him have his way about getting home the way he damn well pleased. Until a couple of days before his reading, I'd had laryngitis. I was going crazy, thinking I'd let him down. At the last minute my voice did come back, and I flew from Virginia to New York and read what I'd written. I think that was the last time I saw him. When David died, I got an e-mail from the director of the Y, who put my intro, and David's reading, up on the site. Sad as it made me, I was transfixed, watching him read, hearing him. Wow: this was David Markson! You put those things out of your mind when you're someone's friend. It isn't willed, you do it automatically. It's clear he did the same with Vonnegut, with Barthelme, with William Gaddis, Harry Mathews, Gilbert Sorrentino. As everyone knows, writers don't talk about what they're writing, and they don't bring up what they've written, either. It's writerly etiquette, writerly superstition, and it's also a way to insist on distance between your writing and who you are. But now that I'm older, I see that those two things aren't necessarily so distinct. You *always* get to be more than the sum of your literary parts, simply because life is complicated and literature is more or less in your control. Other writers understand this, but non-writers don't, which causes writers to skulk around and to avoid cocktail parties (oh yes, this does happen) and to befriend their dry cleaner and maybe, if they're rich, their florist, and of course no different than any non-writer, they love their cats and dogs and miniature ponies, who operate primarily by non-verbal information. No pony ever thought: *This is the author of* Wittgenstein's Mistress.

So I wish he'd had a pony. Or that when he avoided cocktail parties, at least he'd bought better wine for himself. (I suppose he was so perversely proud of not caring what wine tasted like that I shouldn't wish things to be otherwise. Someone he was seeing expressed dismay at his wine choice, so he bought better wine—at least, for her.) He was happy if he ran into a writer friend in the Village when he was out for a walk, maybe on his way to the Strand, which was a place he loved (the feeling was mutual: there was a small table, a sort of David Markson altar, with a review of his book above it and a big pile on the table top.) He was even happier, though, if a tourist asked for directions and he could fill them in, not only about how to get to their destination, but about some of the times *he'd* enjoyed at the tavern they were looking for "years ago."

Though David was polite to tourists, he thought hard about who was really going to become a friend. But he walked—he was Mr. Palomar, with the personal philosophy of Bartleby the Scrivener—and he noticed that all his friends were getting older. The discussions were about health when they stopped to talk. He could complain with the best of them. Some thought he was a hypochondriac. Some of his doctors he liked a lot, some of them he didn't. The doctors and lost tourists—those were the people he'd see, interspersed sometimes with an old friend (Vonnegut was particularly loyal), or he'd have a much anticipated lunch with his son and daughter and his grandchildren. Marvin Paige, who ran Claire's restaurant, was a friend. Burt Britton, formerly at the Strand, then at Books & Co. on Madison. Marvin made up his name. So did Burt. They were whoever they were, but to David they were the fictions Marvin Paige and Burt Britton. So it goes in NYC.

The ageing but *not* financially successful writer who lives in New York City is probably about as rare as Pale Male, the famous hawk who made national news when he built the nest above a swanky uptown apartment building and people were devoted to the sanctity of the birds' rights to nest and to breed and to be left undisturbed. Pale Male was treated a lot more reverently than David Markson—though I'm sure David never aspired to live uptown. (David's own plumage was quite lovely. He favored a black jacket, left unzipped, with a purple lining that really looked startlingly good on him). Like the bird, he just wanted his little place. I was at his small apartment only once, I think. What I remember most is that he'd had many bookcases built, and his books were all neatly arranged, minus their jackets. It was to prevent damage to their jackets, I think. Where did he put them, though? I can't believe I never asked.

In the early eighties, I lived in the attic of a brownstone on West 20th Street, before Chelsea became fashionable. *That* was uptown to David. He gave me the manuscript of *Wittgenstein's Mistress* when he finished it. As any writer will tell you, you just pray that you'll like what another writer hands you. I admit that on rare occasions I've told lies so white, they've been their own little snowstorm— but more often than not, phrased as gently as possible, a writer will tell another writer what he/she thinks. But there was the difference in our ages, I was more often published than he, I'd never read his highly respected book about Malcolm Lowry (and still haven't), I thought some of his books were interesting, others not to my taste. So I welcomed his manuscript, but I was uneasy about beginning to read. When I did, I knew right away, because of the voice, because of how radical, yet simultaneously understated the book was in every way, that it was brilliant. I think it might have taken me a day and a half, but when I called him, I was so filled with admiration that I could barely speak. It's still the most powerful ending of a novel I've ever read, period. Those final words sometimes come to me at the oddest times, driving along, even when I'm on autopilot, grocery shopping. That it was not immediately embraced and celebrated, that he did not become *the* most valued writer, instantly . . . well, I knew all the stories about Melville blah blah blah, and about Fitzgerald dying without knowing *Gatsby* was a classic, but David's book was so overwhelmingly great that I was stunned it got rejected

152

even once, let alone the many, many times it was turned down (I do believe some people were devastated that for one reason or another, they had to say no). What that told me was nothing about the book, but that the so-called literary establishment could not be trusted. I would have tried to sound blasé and say that of course I never trusted it, but until David's experience with that book, I *had* believed, and then Tinkerbell—a lot of Tinkerbells—scattered stardust that stung, that was like sand kicked in your eyes, that truly *hurt*.

What do you say to someone who's written an original, brilliant book that no one will publish? He was darkly humorous enough about the situation for both of us. We kept waiting for the one *Yes*. He was so generous, telling me how much my opinion mattered, and continued to matter. Sometimes I read the rejection letters, or other times he'd read a particularly depressing passage from one to me, over the phone. Something had stepped in between us. Of course neither of us had the power to change anything, but the *thing* was always there. Finally—after way too long—it did get published, and among serious readers, and among writers (who are always serious readers), it's become one of the few texts that, when you say the title, instantly tells other people where you stand. I don't follow the "conversation" on websites and blogs, and I didn't even manage to go to the AWP panel discussion a few years ago. I'm intimidated from both sides: the erudite discussion of David's work that's way beyond me; the memory of who we used to be.

He wasn't kidding when he said he could hardly read fiction at all, after a certain point. I put him in a story once.

I didn't tell him, but I gave him the book. The character was named "Markson" and if he'd seen it, he would certainly have called, or sent me one of his famous, funny postcards. The character wasn't really meant to be him, though the story took place in New York, and the character was at a party to which he or anyone else we knew might have gone. It was a little secret hello from me to him, that's all. He did the same with a line written just for me in one of his books. So I gave the secret wink and he didn't see it, and he gave the secret wink and I smiled. I bring this up because whether overtly or covertly, whether unconsciously, or even as a prank, writers write to other writers. Just because they've died, those writers don't disappear.

Acknowledgments

Many thanks to:

The Poetry Foundation's Harriet blog—for providing both the impetus and the site for my posts on Markson.

Francoise Palleau-Papin, Martha Cooley, and Ann Beattie—fellow Markson friends and champions.

Wes Del Val, the Markson fan and champion whose vision made this book happen, and the rest of the powerHouse team, including Craig Cohen, Will Luckman, and Krzysztof Poluchowicz, who shaped, polished, and perfected.

FARE FORWARD:
Letters from David Markson

Compilation & editing © 2014 Laura Sims
Text © 2014 David Markson used here with permission of his estate

Published in the United States by powerHouse Books,
a division of powerHouse cultural entertainment, Inc.
37 Main Street, Brooklyn, NY 11201-1021
telephone: 212.604.9074, fax: 212.366.5247
email: info@powerHouseBooks.com
website: www.powerHouseBooks.com

First Edition, 2014

Library of Congress Control Number: 2013956378

ISBN 978-1-57687-700-5

Book design by Krzysztof Poluchowicz

Printing and binding through Asia Pacific Offset

A complete catalog of powerHouse Books and limited editions is available upon
request; please call, write, or visit our website.

10 9 8 7 6 5 4 3 2 1

Printed and bound in China